Lace STYLE

Traditional to innovative,
21 inspired designs to knit

Lace Trim

k on RS; p on WS

• p on RS; k on WS

ℓ k1 tbl on both RS and WS

○ yo

↗ p2tog on both RS and WS

╱ k2tog

╲ ssk on RS; p2tog tbl on WS

⅄ k3tog on RS; p3tog on WS

(Lace Trim chart, rows 1–23 odd numbered)

Shape front neck: On the next RS row, knit to last 5 sts, k2tog, k3—1 st dec'd at neck edge (end of RS rows). Dec 1 st at neck edge in this manner every 4th row 8 (6, 4, 4, 2) more times, then every other row 15 (20, 25, 27, 32) times—24 (27, 30, 32, 35) sts total removed by neck shaping.

Shape waist: *At the same time,* when piece measures 9 (9½, 10, 10, 10½)" (23 [24, 25.5, 25.5, 26.5] cm) from CO, inc 1 st at beg of next RS row (side seam edge) as foll: K1, M1, knit to end, including any neck shaping—1 st inc'd. Inc 1 st at side seam edge in this manner every 6th row 4 more times—5 sts total added by waist shaping.

Shape armhole: *Also at the same time,* beg armhole shaping when piece measures 13½ (14, 14½, 14½, 15)" (34 [35.5, 37, 37, 38] cm) from CO, ending with a WS row. BO 4 (4, 4, 5, 6) sts at beg of next RS row, then dec 1 st at armhole edge by working k2, ssk at beg of next 4 (5, 6, 7, 8) RS rows—8 (9, 10, 12, 14) sts total removed by armhole shaping.

When all neck, waist, and armhole shaping have been completed—16 (18, 20, 22, 23) sts rem. Cont even until armhole measures 7 (7½, 8, 8½, 9)" (18 [19, 20.5, 21.5, 23] cm), ending with a WS row.

Shape Shoulder

BO 4 (5, 5, 6, 6) sts at beg of next 2 RS rows, then BO 4 (4, 5, 5, 6) sts at beg of foll RS row, then BO 4 (4, 5, 5, 5) sts at beg of foll RS row.

Dress up plain old garter stitch with a lace edging.

RIGHT FRONT

With A and larger needles, CO 48 (54, 60, 66, 72) sts. Work in garter st for 16 (20, 24, 24, 28) rows, ending with a WS row—piece measures about 2¼ (2¾, 3½, 3½, 4)" (5.5 [7, 9, 9, 10] cm) from CO.

Shape Waist

Next row: (RS) Knit to last 2 sts, k2tog—1 st dec'd. Work 7 rows even. Cont in garter st, rep the shaping of the last 8 rows 4 more times—43 (49, 55, 61, 67) sts rem; piece measures about 8 (8½, 9¼, 9¼, 9¾)" (20.5 [21.5, 23.5, 23.5, 25] cm) from CO. Cont even in garter st until piece measures 8½ (9, 9½, 9½, 10)" (21.5 [23, 24, 24, 25.5] cm), ending with a WS row.

Shape Neck, Waist, and Armholes

Note: The waist increases and armhole shaping are introduced during front neck shaping, and are worked at the same time; read the next three sections all the way through before proceeding.

Shape front neck: On the next RS row, k3, k2tog, knit to end—1 st dec'd at neck edge (beg of RS rows). Dec 1 st at neck edge in this manner every 4th row 8 (6, 4, 4, 2) more times, then every other row 15 (20, 25, 27, 32) times—24 (27, 30, 32, 35) sts total removed by neck shaping.

Shape waist: *At the same time,* when piece measures 9 (9½, 10, 10, 10½)" (23 [24, 25.5, 25.5, 26.5] cm) from CO, inc 1 st at end of next RS row (side seam edge) as foll: Knit to last st, M1, k1—1 st inc'd. Inc 1 st at side seam edge in this manner every 6th row 4 more times—5 sts total added by waist shaping.

Shape armhole: *Also at the same time,* beg armhole shaping when piece measures 13½ (14, 14½, 14½, 15)" (34.5 [35.5, 37, 37, 38] cm) from CO, ending with a RS row. BO 4 (4, 4, 5, 6) sts at beg of next WS row, then dec 1 st at armhole edge by working k2tog, k2 at end of next 4 (5, 6, 7, 8) RS rows—8 (9, 10, 12, 14) sts total removed by armhole shaping.

When all neck, waist, and armhole shaping have been completed—16 (18, 20, 22, 23) sts rem. Cont even until armhole measures 7 (7½, 8, 8½, 9)" (18 [19, 20.5, 21.5, 23] cm), ending with a RS row.

Shape Shoulder

BO 4 (5, 5, 6, 6) sts at beg of next 2 WS rows, then BO 4 (4, 5, 5, 6) sts at beg of foll WS row, then BO 4 (4, 5, 5, 5) sts at beg of foll WS row.

Work fine yarn on large needles to exaggerate lacy effects.

Lace STYLE

Traditional to innovative,
21 inspired designs to knit

PAM ALLEN & ANN BUDD | editors of INTERWEAVE KNITS

INTERWEAVE PRESS
www.interweave.com

PHOTOGRAPHY: **Carol Kaplan**
COVER AND INTERIOR DESIGN: **Jillfrances Gray**

Interweave Press LLC

201 East Fourth Street
Loveland, CO 80537-5655 USA
www.interweave.com

Printed in Singapore by Tien Wah Press

Library of Congress Cataloging-in-Publication Data

Allen, Pam, 1949-
  Lace style : traditional to innovative, 21 inspired designs
to knit / Pam Allen and Ann Budd, authors.
    p. cm.
  Includes bibliographical references and index.
  ISBN-13: 978-1-59668-028-9 (pbk.)
  ISBN-10: 1-59668-028-8 (pbk.)
  1. Knitted lace–Patterns. I. Budd, Ann, 1956- II. Title.
TT805.K54A44 2007
746.43'2041–dc22

2006031041

10 9 8 7 6 5 4 3

ACKNOWLEDGMENTS

For this book and every book in this series, we count ourselves lucky to work with many talented people. We appreciate the skills and creative ideas they've contributed to *Lace Style*.

For their lovely projects, we thank the designers: Véronik Avery, Nancy Bush, Evelyn A. Clark, Kat Coyle, Lisa Daehlin, Norah Gaughan, Priscilla Gibson-Roberts, Annie Modesitt, Michele Rose Orne, Shirley Paden, Mari Lynn Patrick, Mona Schmidt, Vicki Square, Mercedes Tarasovich-Clark, Lois S. Young, Kathy Zimmerman, and Laura Zukaite. Their imagination and dedication to knitting never fail to inspire us.

We're grateful to Lori Gayle, our technical editor, for her clear and concise project patterns, and Veronica Patterson, who polished the text.

As in the two previous books in this series, we thank Jillfrances Gray for her elegant book design; Carol Kaplan for her engaging photographs—and for getting lunch; photo assistant Denise LeBreux, stylist Carrie Hoge, and Lisa Evans for keeping things organized and moving along; and models Maureen Emerson, Caitlin FitzGerald, Sabrina Seelig, and Kara Shorno for gracefully wearing wool sweaters on the hottest day in July.

Finally, we are indebted to Sherry Gibson at Black Parrot in Rockland, Maine, and Denise Novotny and Missy Tasker at Simply Chic, and Angie Bibeau at Bliss in Portland, Maine, for their generosity in lending us garments for styling. Also, warmest thanks to the people who provided locations: Julia and Walter Clay for their house and vintage convertible; Susanna Crampton at Historic New England; and Elizabeth Farish, Ann Pilgrim, and Melissa Scott at the Hamilton House for their gracious welcome and the cooling fans that kept us comfortable.

CONTENTS

THE INTRIGUE OF LACE

Knitted lace has a long history. The delicate tracery of openings that both veil and reveal what lies beneath has beguiled knitters for centuries. Although a fabric designed around patterns of eyelets or holes hasn't the warmth or insulating properties of solid stockinette stitch, knitters have incorporated hundreds of lace patterns into their work simply to enjoy the delicate beauty of lace and experience the pleasure that comes from knitting it.

Following the format of *Scarf Style* and *Wrap Style*, *Lace Style* is a book about knitting lace as well as a book of lace projects to knit. It's a collection of patterns from eighteen talented and inventive knitwear designers from across the country, each of whom has incorporated holes into knitted fabric in her own, unique way. Every design offers an individual lesson in inspiration, technique, application, and of course, style. As a collection, the patterns will give you new ways to think about knitting lace and provide you with endless creative possibilities.

Whether you're new to knitting lace or have been knitting lace forever, you'll want to spend some time with the Design Notebook (page 130). From the Notebook, you can learn how to make yarnover increases and various types of decreases that interact with one another to produce the openwork patterns we call lace. You'll discover ways to get the look of lace without knitting a single increase or decrease. You'll also learn how to read lace charts, incorporate lace motifs into your own designs, block your lace projects, and avoid (or fix) lace-knitting errors.

At the end of *Lace Style*, you'll find a glossary of terms and techniques that includes illustrated instructions for all the specific techniques mentioned in the projects. Along with the easy-to-follow directions and clear illustrations in the project and design chapters, the glossary will provide the help you need to successfully complete any project in this book.

So get some yarn, grab your needles, and knit up some holes.

. . . the patterns will give you new ways to think about knitting lace . . .

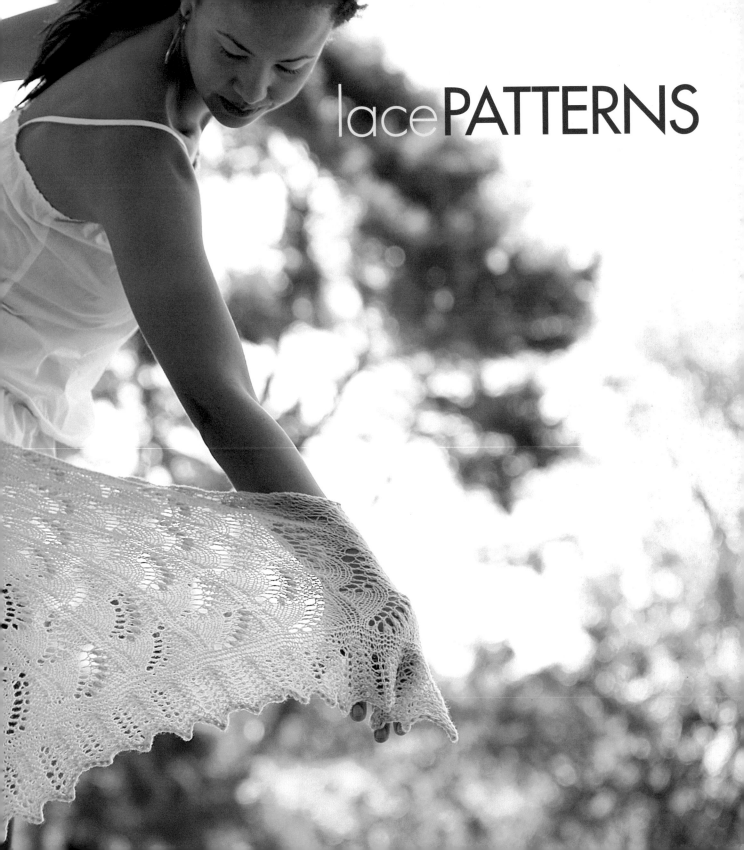

lacePATTERNS

Sometimes two yarns are better than one—especially when they're two weights of the same luscious alpaca—as **Mari Lynn Patrick** demonstrates in this wear-everywhere wrap jacket. Mari Lynn used a DK-weight yarn for the garter stitch body and sleeves, then knitted a large-scale edging in a lighter weight yarn for the fold-over front edges and collar. The delicate lace provides an interesting contrast to the rustic garter stitch, and is echoed in a small eyelet detail on the cuffs. Garter stitch ties hold the wrap closed at the waist.

BACK

With A and larger needles, CO 70 (78, 86, 96, 104) sts. Work in garter st (knit every row) for 16 (20, 24, 24, 28) rows, ending with a WS row—piece measures about 2¼ (2¾, 3½, 3½, 4)" (5.5 [7, 9, 9, 10] cm) from CO.

Shape Waist

Row 1: (RS) K23 (26, 28, 32, 34), place marker (pm), sl 1, k2tog, psso, k18 (20, 24, 26, 30), sl 1, k2tog, psso, pm, k23 (26, 28, 32, 34)—66 (74, 82, 92, 100) sts rem.

Rows 2–10: Knit.

Row 11: (RS) Knit to first m, slip marker (sl m), sl 1, k2tog, psso, knit to 3 sts before next m, sl 1, k2tog, psso, sl m, knit to end—4 sts dec'd.

Rows 12–41: Rep Rows 2–11 three more times—50 (58, 66, 76, 84) sts rem; piece measures about 8¼ (8¾, 9¼, 9¼, 9¾)" (21 [22, 23.5, 23.5, 25] cm) from CO.

Cont even in garter st until piece measures 9 (9½, 10, 10, 10½)" (23 [24, 25.5, 25.5, 26.5] cm) from CO, ending with a WS row. *Inc row:* (RS) Knit to first m, sl m, M1 (see Glossary, page 155), knit to next m, M1, sl m, knit to end—2 sts inc'd. Work 3 rows even in garter st. Cont in garter st, rep the last 4 rows 7 more times—66 (74, 82, 92, 100) sts. Cont even in garter st until piece measures 13½ (14, 14½, 14½, 15)" (34.5 [35.5, 37, 37, 38] cm) from CO, ending with a WS row.

Shape Armholes

BO 4 (4, 4, 5, 6) sts at beg of next 2 rows—58 (66, 74, 82, 88) sts rem. Dec 1 st each end of needle on next RS row as foll: K2, ssk, knit to last 4 sts, k2tog, k2—2 sts dec'd. Dec 1 st each end of needle in this manner every RS row 3 (4, 5, 6, 7) more times—50 (56, 62, 68, 72) sts rem. Cont even until armholes measure 7 (7½, 8, 8½, 9)" (18 [19, 20.5, 21.5, 23] cm), ending with a WS row.

FINISHED SIZE
32 (35½, 39½, 44, 48)" (81.5 [90, 100.5, 112, 122] cm) bust circumference, tied. Jacket shown measures 32" (81.5 cm).

YARN
DK weight (CYCA #3 Light) for body (A); sportweight (CYCA #2 Fine) for lace trim (B).

Shown here: Plymouth Indiecita Baby Alpaca DK (100% alpaca; 125 yd [114 m]/50 g): #207 light beige (A), 8 (9, 11, 12, 13) balls.

Plymouth Indiecita 3 Ply Sport (100% alpaca; 185 yd [169 m]/50 g): #207 light beige (B), 2 (2, 3, 3, 3) balls.

NEEDLES
Body and sleeves—size 10 (6 mm): straight. Sleeve cuffs and lace trim—size 8 (5 mm): straight. Adjust needle sizes if necessary to obtain correct gauge.

NOTIONS
Markers (m); tapestry needle.

GAUGE
25 stitches = 6" (15 cm) and 28 rows = 4" (10 cm) in garter st with DK-weight yarn on larger needles. Lace trim measures 5½" (14 cm) at widest point; 24 rows of lace trim = 3½" (9 cm) high with sportweight yarn on smaller needles.

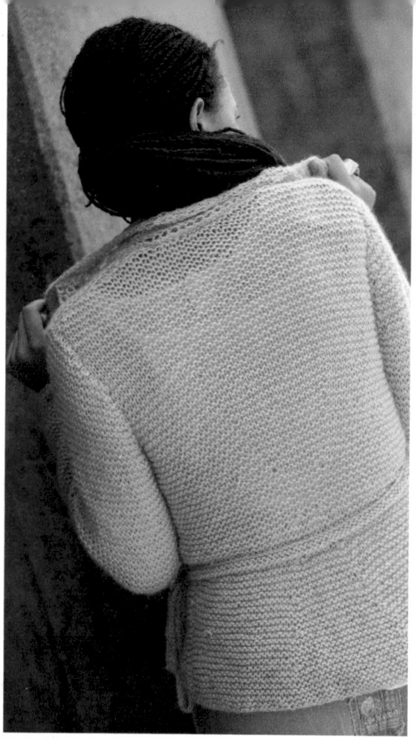

Shape Shoulders

BO 4 (5, 5, 6, 6) sts at beg of next 4 rows, then BO 4 (4, 5, 5, 6) sts at beg of foll 2 rows, then BO 4 (4, 5, 5, 5) sts at beg of foll 2 rows—18 (20, 22, 24, 26) sts rem. BO all sts.

LEFT FRONT

With A and larger needles, CO 48 (54, 60, 66, 72) sts. Work in garter st for 16 (20, 24, 24, 28) rows, ending with a WS row—piece measures about 2¼ (2¾, 3½, 3½, 4)" (5.5 [7, 9, 9, 10] cm) from CO.

Shape Waist

Next row: (RS) K2tog, knit to end—1 st dec'd. Work 7 rows even. Cont in garter st, rep the shaping of the last 8 rows 4 more times—43 (49, 55, 61, 67) sts rem; piece measures about 8 (8½, 9¼, 9¼, 9¾)" (20.5 [21.5, 23.5, 23.5, 25] cm) from CO. Cont even in garter st until piece measures 8½ (9, 9½, 9½, 10)" (21.5 [23, 24, 24, 25.5] cm), ending with a WS row.

Shape Neck, Waist, and Armholes

Note: The waist increases and armhole shaping are introduced during front neck shaping, and are worked at the same time; read the next three sections all the way through before proceeding.

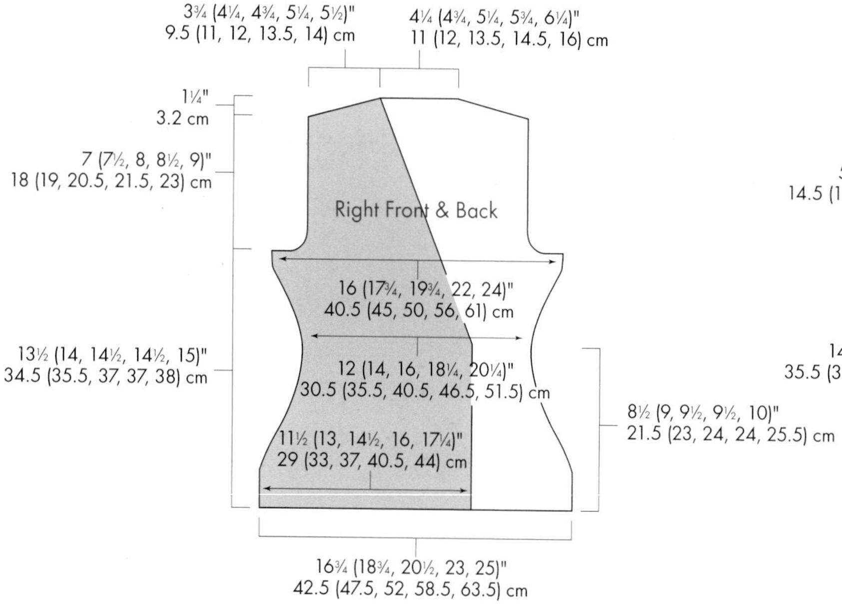
3¾ (4¼, 4¾, 5¼, 5½)"
9.5 (11, 12, 13.5, 14) cm
4¼ (4¾, 5¼, 5¾, 6¼)"
11 (12, 13.5, 14.5, 16) cm
1¼"
3.2 cm
7 (7½, 8, 8½, 9)"
18 (19, 20.5, 21.5, 23) cm
Right Front & Back
16 (17¾, 19¾, 22, 24)"
40.5 (45, 50, 56, 61) cm
13½ (14, 14½, 14½, 15)"
34.5 (35.5, 37, 37, 38) cm
12 (14, 16, 18¼, 20¼)"
30.5 (35.5, 40.5, 46.5, 51.5) cm
8½ (9, 9½, 9½, 10)"
21.5 (23, 24, 24, 25.5) cm
11½ (13, 14½, 16, 17¼)"
29 (33, 37, 40.5, 44) cm
16¾ (18¾, 20½, 23, 25)"
42.5 (47.5, 52, 58.5, 63.5) cm

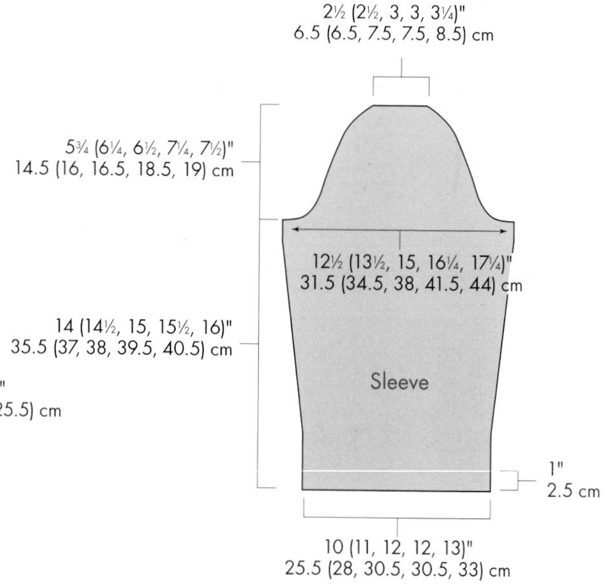
2½ (2½, 3, 3, 3¼)"
6.5 (6.5, 7.5, 7.5, 8.5) cm
5¾ (6¼, 6½, 7¼, 7½)"
14.5 (16, 16.5, 18.5, 19) cm
12½ (13½, 15, 16¼, 17¼)"
31.5 (34.5, 38, 41.5, 44) cm
14 (14½, 15, 15½, 16)"
35.5 (37, 38, 39.5, 40.5) cm
Sleeve
1"
2.5 cm
10 (11, 12, 12, 13)"
25.5 (28, 30.5, 30.5, 33) cm

SLEEVES

With B and smaller needles, CO 7 sts (all sizes).

Row 1: (RS) K4, yo, p2tog, k1.

Row 2: K3, yo, p2tog, k2.

Rep Rows 1 and 2 until piece measures 10 (11, 12, 12, 13)" (25.5 [28, 30.5, 30.5, 33] cm) from CO. BO all sts. Hold sleeve edging horizontally with RS facing and the long edge nearer to the yarnovers across the top. With A and larger needles, pick up and knit 40 (46, 50, 50, 54) sts along long edge of strip. Cont in garter st, inc 1 st each end of needle every 12th row 2 (5, 6, 6, 6) times, then every 10th row 4 (0, 0, 3, 3) times—52 (56, 62, 68, 72) sts. Work even until piece measures 14 (14½, 15, 15½, 16)" (35.5 [37, 38, 39.5, 40.5] cm) from lower selvedge of sleeve edging, ending with a WS row.

Shape Cap

BO 4 (4, 4, 5, 6) sts at beg of next 2 rows—44 (48, 54, 58, 60) sts rem. Dec 1 st each end of needle on next RS row as foll: K2, ssk, knit to last 4 sts, k2tog, k2—2 sts dec'd. Dec 1 st each end of needle in this manner every RS row 2 (4, 7, 9, 8) more times, then every *other* RS row 6 (6, 5, 5, 6) times—26 (26, 28, 28, 30) sts rem. BO 2 sts at beg of next 8 rows—10 (10, 12, 12, 14) sts rem. BO all sts.

FINISHING

Ties (make 2)

With A and smaller needles, CO 152 (170, 186, 208, 224) sts. Work in garter st for 4 rows. BO all sts.

Lace Trim

With B and smaller needles, CO 17 sts. Rep Rows 1–24 of Lace Trim chart (see page 15) 14 (15, 16, 16, 17) times—piece measures about 49 (52½, 56, 56, 59½)" (124.5 [133.5, 142, 142, 151] cm) from CO. Loosely BO all sts. Block, pinning each point to create a defined edge.

With A threaded on a tapestry needle, sew fronts to back at shoulders. Pin straight selvedge of lace trim along the front opening, easing in any fullness, and with the WS of the lace trim corresponding to the RS of the garment so that RS of trim will show when it is folded back. With B threaded on a tapestry needle, sew lace trim in place around front opening. Fold lace trim back and sew ties to fronts along seam between lace trim and front edge and even with beg of neck shaping. Sew side seams, leaving a 1" (2.5 cm) opening at the waist in the right side seam for the tie. Sew sleeve caps into armholes. Sew sleeve seams. Weave in loose ends. To wear, thread left tie through hole in right side seam, bring both ties around to the back, cross ties in back, and tie at the side.

For centuries, a white lace blouse has been a wardrobe staple, but when that blouse is covered with a jacket, all that shows are the cuffs. With this notion in mind, **Vicki Square** designed a pair of mohair cuffs that can be worn with any garment. The cuffs are worked in the round from the pointy edge of the lace to the snug rib that fits around the wrist. The lace portion is a simple six-stitch pattern that repeats every two rows. And every other row is knitted plain. Tuck these cuffs under the sleeves of a blazer or dress for a lacy layered look.

STITCH GUIDE

Lace Pattern: (multiple of 6 sts)
Rnd 1: *K1, yo, k1, sl 1, k2tog, psso, k1, yo; rep from * to end of rnd.
Rnd 2: Knit.
Repeat Rnds 1 and 2 for pattern.

CUFF

Loosely CO 72 sts. Divide sts evenly onto 3 dpn (24 sts on each needle) and join for working in the rnd, being careful not to twist sts. Rep Rnds 1 and 2 of lace patt (see Stitch Guide) until piece measures 5½" (14 cm) from CO, ending with Rnd 2. *Note:* Be careful that you do not accidentally drop any yo that occurs at the end of a needle or at the end of the rnd. *Dec rnd:* *K2tog; rep from * to end of rnd—36 sts rem. *Next rnd:* *K2, p2; rep from * to end of rnd. Cont in k2, p2 rib as established until ribbed section measures 2½" (6.5 cm) and cuff measures about 8" (20.5 cm) from CO. Loosely BO all sts.

FINISHING

Weave in loose ends. Block lightly if desired as foll: Generously spritz inside and outside of lace portion with a fine mist. Lay cuff on ironing board or padded surface with scalloped edges of both layers aligned. Pin CO edge to about 7" (18 cm) wide, then pin out each scallop point, pulling gently downward to extend points and to expand and even out the lace patt. When scallop points have been pinned, coax the valley between pairs of points upward toward the ribbing to exaggerate zigzag lower edge, and pin valleys in place. Allow upper section of lace cuff to narrow gradually to width of ribbing. Allow to air-dry completely before removing pins.

FINISHED SIZE
About 6" (15 cm) wrist circumference and 8" (20.5 cm) long. Ribbing at wrist will stretch to about 8" (20.5 cm) circumference.

YARN
Sportweight (CYCA #2 Fine).
Shown here: Filatura Di Crosa Baby Kid Extra (80% mohair kid, 20% nylon; 268 yd [245 m]/25 g): #310 ivory, 1 ball.

NEEDLES
Size 6 (4 mm): set of 4 or 5 double-pointed (dpn). Adjust needle size if necessary to obtain the correct gauge.

NOTIONS
Tapestry needle.

GAUGE
24 stitches and 19 rounds = 4" (10 cm) in lace pattern worked in the round.

LILY OF THE VALLEY SHAWL
NANCY BUSH

Some of the most beautiful lace patterns come from Eastern Europe. The lily of the valley pattern **Nancy Bush** used in this shawl is a traditional but enduringly popular motif that originated in Estonia. Nancy's shawl is worked as a large rectangle with sprigs of lily of the valley accented with the characteristic *nupps* (buds or buttons) that alternate with sprigs without nupps. Every other row is purled to produce a smooth stockinette-stitch background that doesn't interfere with the lace pattern. The edging, however, is worked with a garter stitch background in rounds that grow outward from the edges of the rectangle and end with sharp points along the bind-off edge.

STITCH GUIDE

Nupp: Working very loosely, work [k1, yo, k1, yo, k1] all in same st—5 nupp sts made from 1 st. On the foll row, purl these 5 sts tog to dec to 1 st. *Note:* The initial nupp sts must be worked more loosely than customary in order to work them as p5tog on the next row.

FINISHED SIZE
About 23" (58.5 cm) wide and 60" (152.5 cm) long.

YARN
Lace weight (no CYCA equivalent).
Shown here: Jaggerspun Superfine Merino (100% merino; 630 yd [576 m]/2 oz): mushroom (pale grayish taupe), 2 skeins.

NEEDLES
Size 6 (4 mm): straight and 32" (80 cm) circular (cir). Adjust needle size if necessary to obtain the correct gauge.

NOTIONS
Several yards of sport- or worsted-weight cotton in contrasting color for provisional cast-on; markers (m; 1 in a color or style different from the others); size G/6 (4 mm) crochet hook; tapestry needle.

GAUGE
24 sts and 30 rnds = 4" (10 cm) in stockinette stitch worked in the round before blocking.

CENTER RECTANGLE

With crochet hook and contrasting yarn, make a crochet chain (see Glossary, page 154) about 110 loops long. Cut yarn, pull the tail through the last chain loop, and tie a knot or loop in this tail so you can find it later when you want to remove the cast-on. With main yarn and using the crochet chain provisional technique (see Glossary, page 152), pick up and knit 100 sts in the back loop "bumps" on the underside of the crochet chain, beg and ending 5 ch sts from each end.

Row 1: (WS) K1 (edge st), k3 (garter "frame" sts), place marker (pm), k92, pm, k3 (garter frame sts), k1 (edge st).

Row 2: (RS) Sl 1 pwise with yarn in front (wyf), bring yarn to back, knit to end of row.

Row 3: Sl 1 pwise wyf (edge st), bring yarn to back, knit to last st, k1tbl (edge st).

Rows 4–7: Rep Row 3 four more times, ending with a WS row—4 garter st ridges completed.

Change to Lily of the Valley chart, and work in patt from chart until Rows 1–28 have been repeated 10 times, then work Rows 1–14 once more—294 patt rows total. *Next row:* (RS) Sl 1 pwise wyf, knit to last st, k1tbl. Rep the last row 7 more times—4 garter ridges completed. Do not cut yarn.

Legend

☐	k on RS; p on WS
•	k on WS
⅄	sl 1 pwise wyf on RS and WS
℞	k1 tbl on RS and WS
O	yo
∕	k2tog
＼	sl 1 kwise, k1, psso
⋌	sl 1 kwise, k2tog, psso
⅏	nupp (see Stitch Guide)
⑤	p5tog on WS
▨	no stitch
☐	pattern repeat
☐	corner stitch
┃	corner marker position

Lily of the Valley

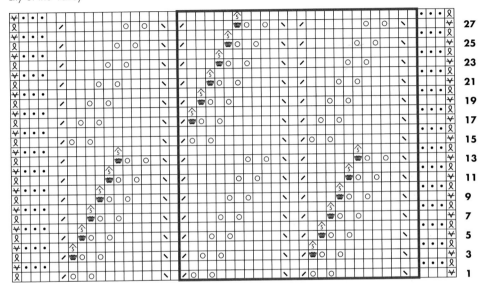

27
25
23
21
19
17
15
13
11
9
7
5
3
1

Edging

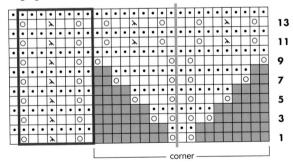

13
11
9
7
5
3
1

corner

There's nothing "old fashioned" about old lace patterns.

EDGING

(*Note:* Pick up sts for edging along the chained selvedges as foll: Pick up 1 st in the first selvedge chain st by inserting the needle tip under both legs of the st, pick up 1 st in the back half of the second chain by inserting the needle tip under only the back leg of that chain, then pick up 1 st from the same whole chain by inserting the needle tip under both legs—3 sts picked up from 2 chain selvedge sts). Change to cir needle. K1 (corner st), place different-color marker to indicate beg of rnd, knit to end, inc 14 sts evenly spaced and removing other markers as you come them—114 sts. With the RS of piece still facing, pick up and knit 234 sts along one long side, pm after the first picked-up st (corner st)—348 sts total; if you have made any length adjustments, make sure the number of sts picked up along the selvedge is a multiple of 8 plus 2. Carefully undo the marked end of the crochet chain, pull gently to unzip, and place live sts on needle as they become free—100 sts released from CO edge. Knit the first freed st (corner st), pm, knit to end inc 14 sts evenly spaced—462 sts. Pick up and knit 234 sts along rem long side, pm after the first picked up st (corner st)—696 sts; 4 corner sts, each with

a marker immediately after it; first corner st of rnd marked with a different color; if you have made length adjustments, be sure to pick up the same number of sts as for the other side. Work Rnd 1 of Edging chart as foll: *On the first short side, k1 (corner st), slip marker (sl m), yo, [k1, yo, k2, sl 1 kwise, k2tog, psso, k2, yo] 14 times, k1, yo (shown as first st on chart, before center st). On the first long side, k1 (corner st), sl m, yo, [k1, yo, k2, sl 1 kwise, k2tog, psso, k2, yo] 29 times, k1, yo (first st of chart). Rep from * for the rem short and long sides to complete Rnd 1 of chart—2 sts inc'd at each corner; 8 sts inc'd total. For Rnd 2 of chart, purl all sts. Cont until Rnd 14 of chart has been completed—768 sts. Join a second strand of yarn, and BO with 2 strands held tog as foll: Sl 1 pwise, *k1, insert left needle tip into front of these 2 sts from left to right and knit them tog; rep from * until last 2 sts have been knitted tog, cut yarn, and pull through last st to fasten off.

FINISHING

Block shawl to about 28" (71 cm) wide and 66" (167.5 cm) long by pinning the damp shawl on a towel; piece will relax to about 23" (58.5 cm) wide and 60" (152.5 cm) long when unpinned. Start by stretching each corner to the blocking measurements, then work from side to side, pinning out the "points" at the top of the [yo, k1, yo] columns of the edging. Allow to completely air-dry before removing pins. Weave in loose ends.

Evelyn A. Clark nearly always has a pair of socks on her needles. And a good number of those socks include a lace pattern along the leg and top of the foot. In this pair, she worked a small scalloped lace border that evolves into columns of little lace flowers. The simple stitch pattern, which she discovered in a Burda pattern book, repeats over eight rounds, five of which are knit-one-purl-one ribs that provide elasticity for a snug fit. Knitted in a silk sock yarn, these anklets are dressy and durable.

NOTE
❖ When measuring the length of the leg or foot, stretch the lace pattern widthwise slightly, about enough to make the purl columns in the floral lace and instep floral lace patterns visible between the knit columns.

STITCH GUIDE

Border Pattern: (multiple of 6 sts)
Rnd 1: Purl.
Rnds 2 and 4: *P1, k5; rep from *.
Rnd 3: *P1, yo, k1, sl 1, k2tog, psso, k1, yo; rep from *.
Rnd 5: *P1, k1, yo, sl 1, k2tog, psso, yo, k1; rep from *.
Rnd 6: *P1, k5; rep from *.
Repeat Rnds 1–6 for pattern.

Floral Lace Pattern: (multiple of 6 sts)
Rnds 1–4: *P1, k1; rep from *.
Rnd 5: *P1, yo, ssk, k1, k2tog, yo; rep from *.
Rnd 6: *P1, k5; rep from *.
Rnd 7: *P1, k1, yo, sl 1, k2tog, psso, yo, k1; rep from *.
Rnd 8: *P1, k1; rep from *.
Repeat Rnds 1–8 for pattern.

Instep Floral Lace Pattern: (multiple of 6 sts + 1)
Rnds 1–4: *P1, k1; rep from * to last st, p1.
Rnd 5: *P1, yo, ssk, k1, k2tog, yo; rep from * to last st, p1.
Rnd 6: *P1, k5; rep from * to last st, p1.
Rnd 7: *P1, k1, yo, sl 1, k2tog, psso, yo, k1; rep from * to last st, p1.
Rnd 8: *P1, k1; rep from * to last st, p1.
Repeat Rnds 1–8 for pattern.

FINISHED SIZE
About 7" (18 cm) foot circumference unstretched, and 9½" (24 cm) foot length from back of heel to tip of toe. To fit about women's U.S. shoe sizes 7 to 8½. *Note:* Socks will stretch to accommodate up to about 9½" (24 cm) foot circumference.

YARN
Fingering weight (CYCA #1 Super Fine).
Shown here: Regia Silk (55% merino, 25% polyamide, 20% silk; 219 yd [200 m]/ 50 g): #54 smoke (light blue), 2 balls.

NEEDLES
Size 1 (2.25 mm): set of 4 double-pointed (dpn). Adjust needle size if necessary to obtain the correct gauge.

NOTIONS
Marker (m); tapestry needle.

GAUGE
18 stitches and 26 rounds = 2" (5 cm) in stockinette stitch worked in the round.

LEG

Loosely CO 60 sts. Divide sts on 3 dpn so that there are 18 sts on Needle 1, 18 sts on Needle 2, and 24 sts on Needle 3. Place marker (pm) and join for working in the rnd, being careful not to twist sts. Purl 1 rnd. Work Rnds 1–6 of border patt (see Stitch Guide) once, then rep Rnds 3–6 *only* 2 more times—14 rnds total. Change to floral lace patt (see Stitch Guide) and rep Rnds 1–8 of patt 6 times total—piece measures about 4½" (11.5 cm) from CO, slightly stretched (see Note).

HEEL

Heel Flap

Turn work so WS is facing. Sl 1 pwise with yarn in back (wyb), p28—29 heel sts; rem 31 sts will be worked later for instep. Work 29 heel sts back and forth in rows as foll:

Row 1: (RS) *Sl 1 pwise wyb, k1; rep from * to last st, k1.

Row 2: (WS) Sl 1 pwise wyb, purl to end.

Rep Rows 1 and 2 sixteen more times, then work RS Row 1 once more—36 rows total, including first WS row; flap measures about 2¼" (5.5 cm).

Shape Heel

Work short-rows as foll:

Row 1: (WS) Sl 1, p15, p2tog, p1, turn work.

Row 2: (RS) Sl 1, k4, ssk, k1, turn.

Row 3: Sl 1, p5, p2tog, p1, turn.

Row 4: Sl 1, k6, ssk, k1, turn.

Row 5: Sl 1, p7, p2tog, p1, turn.

Row 6: Sl 1, k8, ssk, k1, turn.

Row 7: Sl 1, p9, p2tog, p1, turn.

Row 8: Sl 1, k10, ssk, k1, turn.

Row 9: Sl 1, p11, p2tog, p1, turn.

Row 10: Sl 1, k12, ssk, k1, turn.

Row 11: Sl 1, p13, p2tog, p1, turn.

Row 12: Sl 1, k14, ssk, k1—17 heel sts rem.

Shape Gusset

Pick up sts along edges of heel flap and rejoin for working in the rnd as foll:

Rnd 1: With Needle 1, pick up and knit 19 sts along side edge of heel flap; with Needle 2 work Rnd 1 of instep floral lace patt (see Stitch Guide) over 31 instep sts; with Needle 3, pick up and knit 19 sts along other side edge of heel flap, then knit the first 9 heel sts. Sl rem 8 heel sts to beg of Needle 1—86 sts total; 27 sts on Needle 1, 31 instep sts on Needle 2, 28 sts on Needle 3. Rnd begins at center of heel.

Rnd 2: On Needle 1, working through the back loops of the pick-up sts, knit to last 2 sts, k2tog; on Needle 2, cont in established lace patt; on Needle 3, ssk, knit to end, working through the back loops of the picked-up sts—2 sts dec'd.

Rnd 3: On Needle 1, knit; on Needle 2, cont in established lace patt; on Needle 3, knit. Rep Rnds 2 and 3 twelve more times—60 sts rem; 14 sts on Needle 1, 31 sts on Needle 2, 15 sts on Needle 3.

FOOT

Cont even in patt as established until piece measures 8" (20.5 cm) from back of heel when slightly stretched, or about 1½" (3.8 cm) less than desired total foot length, ending with Rnd 8 of lace patt. For most accurate fit, try sock on wearer's foot.

TOE

Working in St st, shape toe as foll:
Rnd 1: On Needle 1, k14, then k1 from beg of Needle 2; on Needle 2, k30; on Needle 3, k15—15 sts each on Needle 1 and Needle 3, 30 sts on Needle 2.
Rnd 2: On Needle 1, knit to last 3 sts, k2tog, k1; on Needle 2, k1, ssk, knit to last 3 sts, k2tog, k1; on Needle 3, k1, ssk, knit to end—4 sts dec'd.
Rnd 3: Knit.
Rep Rnds 2 and 3 six more times—32 sts rem; 8 sts each on Needle 1 and Needle 3, 16 sts on Needle 2. Rep Rnd 2 *every* rnd 4 times—16 sts rem; 4 sts each on Needle 1 and Needle 3, 8 sts on Needle 2. Knit sts from Needle 1 onto the end of Needle 3—8 sts each on 2 needles.

FINISHING

Break yarn, leaving a 12" (30.5 cm) tail. Thread tail on a tapestry needle and use the Kitchener st (see Glossary, page 155) to graft sts tog. Weave in loose ends. Block lightly.

Raise the lowly sock to a high-fashion accessory with a pretty lace pattern.

LACE-EDGED CORSET
MICHELE ROSE ORNE

Michele Rose Orne is an expert in designing sophisticated feminine knitwear. In this delicate corset top, she chose a silk yarn for the body and a very fine, crisp cotton yarn for the delicate lace edging at the neck and hem. The rounded lower front edge is shaped by casting on stitches at each side. A series of darts on the bodice front as well as narrow ribs with lots of tiny buttons on the bodice back give the top a snug fit. A drawstring holds the scoop neck in place.

STITCH GUIDE

Right Twist (RT): K2tog, but do not slip sts from left needle, knit the first st again, then slip both sts off needle.

LEFT BACK

With MC, CO 59 (67, 73, 81, 87) sts.

Decrease for Waist

Row 1: (RS) K3, p2, [k2, p2] 6 times, k14 (18, 21, 25, 28), knit the next st and mark it for dart shaping by placing a removable marker or safety pin in the st itself (not between sts on the needle), k15 (19, 22, 26, 29). *Note:* Move the removable marker up every few rows as you work so you can always easily identify the marked st.

Rows 2–8: Cont as established (knit the knits and purl the purls as they appear).

Row 9: (dec row) K3, p2, [k2, p2] 6 times, knit to 1 st before marked st, sl 2 tog kwise, k1, p2sso, knit to end—2 sts dec'd; marked dart st is center st of the double dec.

Rows 10–14: Work 5 rows even as established.

Rows 15–32: Rep Rows 9–14 three more times—51 (59, 65, 73, 79) sts rem.

Row 33: Rep Row 9—49 (57, 63, 71, 77) sts rem.

Work 13 (17, 17, 21, 21) rows even as established, ending with a WS row—piece measures about 5 (5½, 5½, 6, 6)" (12.5 [14, 14, 15, 15] cm) from CO, measured straight up along a single column of sts; do not measure along the curved dart line.

FINISHED SIZE

34 (38, 42, 46, 50)" (86.5 [96.5, 106.5, 117, 127] cm) bust circumference.

YARN

Sportweight (CYCA #2 Fine); #10 pearl cotton (no CYCA equivalent).

Shown here: Sirdar Schulana Seta Bella Silk (100% silk; 125 yd [114 m]/50 g): #12 natural (MC), 5 (5, 6, 7, 8) balls.

Scheiller+Stahl Manuela Hakelgarn #10 cotton (100% mercerized cotton): #M026 cream (CC), 1 (1, 2, 2, 2) balls.

NEEDLES

Size 3 (3.25 mm): straight. Adjust needle size if necessary to obtain the correct gauge.

NOTIONS

Markers (m); removable markers or safety pins; stitch holders; tapestry needle; ⅜" (1 cm) crystal or pearl buttons, 19 (21, 22, 24, 25) for closely spaced buttons if placed in every yarnover hole in buttonhole band, or 10 (11, 11, 12, 13) buttons if placed in every other yarnover hole.

GAUGE

28 stitches and 36 rows = 4" (10 cm) in stockinette stitch using MC; 32 stitches and 36 rows = 4" (10 cm) in k2, p2 rib panels for back with MC with rib slightly stretched so that p2 columns appear 1 st wide.

Increase for Waist

Row 1: K3, p2, [k2, p2] 6 times, knit to marked st, M1 (see Glossary, page 155), k1 (marked st), M1, knit to end—2 sts inc'd.

Rows 2–8: Work 7 rows even as established.

Rows 9–32: Rep Rows 1–8 three more times—57 (65, 71, 79, 85) sts.

Row 33: Rep Row 1—59 (67, 73, 81, 87) sts.

Cont even as established until piece measures 9½ (10, 10½, 11, 11½)" (24 [25.5, 26.5, 28, 29] cm) from CO, ending with a RS row.

Shape Armhole and Neck

Cont in patt as established, BO 4 (5, 5, 6, 6) sts at beg of next WS row, then BO 3 (3, 4, 4, 4) sts at beg of foll 2 WS rows, then BO 0 (0, 3, 3, 3) sts at beg foll 0 (0, 1, 1, 1) WS row, then BO 2 sts at beg of foll WS row, then BO 1 st at beg of foll 1 (2, 3, 4, 5) WS row(s)—46 (52, 52, 58, 63) sts rem; armhole measures about 1 (1¼, 1¾, 2, 2¼)" (2.5 [3.2, 4.5, 5, 5.5] cm). Work even in patt until armhole measures 1½ (1¾, 2¼, 2½, 2¾)" (3.8 [4.5, 5.5, 6.5, 7] cm), ending with a WS row. Cont in patt, BO 25 (28, 28, 31, 34) sts at beg of next RS row, then BO 8 (9, 9, 10, 11) sts at beg of foll RS row, then BO 5 (6, 6, 6, 7) sts at beg of foll RS row, then BO 2 (2, 2, 3, 3) sts at beg of foll RS row, then BO 1 st at beg of foll 2 (3, 3, 4, 4) RS rows—4 sts rem; armhole measures about 2¾ (3¼, 3¾, 4¼, 4½)" (7 [8.5, 9.5, 11, 11.5] cm). Place sts on holder to be worked later for strap.

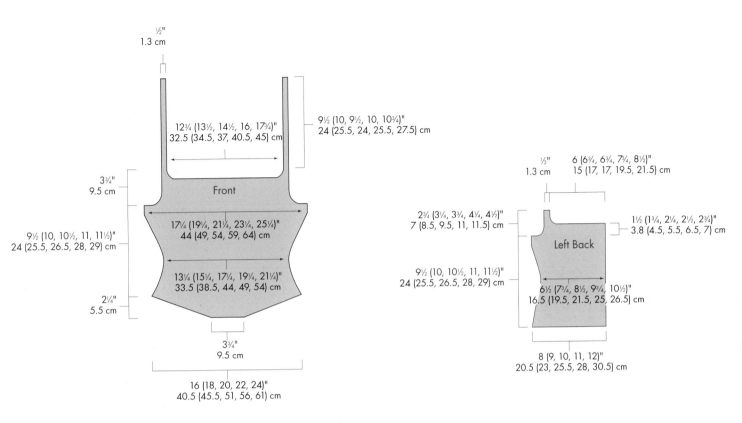

Front

½"
1.3 cm

12¾ (13½, 14½, 16, 17¾)"
32.5 (34.5, 37, 40.5, 45) cm

9½ (10, 9½, 10, 10¾)"
24 (25.5, 24, 25.5, 27.5) cm

3¾"
9.5 cm

17¼ (19¼, 21¼, 23¼, 25¼)"
44 (49, 54, 59, 64) cm

9½ (10, 10½, 11, 11½)"
24 (25.5, 26.5, 28, 29) cm

13¼ (15¼, 17¼, 19¼, 21¼)"
33.5 (38.5, 44, 49, 54) cm

2¼"
5.5 cm

3¾"
9.5 cm

16 (18, 20, 22, 24)"
40.5 (45.5, 51, 56, 61) cm

Left Back

½"
1.3 cm

6 (6¾, 6¾, 7¾, 8½)"
15 (17, 17, 19.5, 21.5) cm

2¾ (3¼, 3¾, 4¼, 4½)"
7 (8.5, 9.5, 11, 11.5) cm

1½ (1¾, 2¼, 2½, 2¾)"
3.8 (4.5, 5.5, 6.5, 7) cm

9½ (10, 10½, 11, 11½)"
24 (25.5, 26.5, 28, 29) cm

6½ (7¾, 8½, 9¾, 10½)"
16.5 (19.5, 21.5, 25, 26.5) cm

8 (9, 10, 11, 12)"
20.5 (23, 25.5, 28, 30.5) cm

RIGHT BACK

Note: The rib section of right back has 7 more sts than left back so finished buttonhole band of left back will overlap right back.

With MC, CO 66 (74, 80, 88, 94) sts.

Decrease for Waist

Row 1: (RS) K15 (19, 22, 26, 29), knit the next st and mark it for dart shaping by placing a removable marker or safety pin in the st itself (not between sts on the needle), k14 (18, 21, 25, 28), [p2, k2] 9 times.

Rows 2–8: Cont as established (knit the knits and purl the purls as they appear).

Row 9: (dec row) Knit to 1 st before marked st, sl 2 tog kwise, k1, p2sso, work as established to end—2 sts dec'd; marked dart st is center st of the double dec.

Rows 10–14: Work 5 rows even as established.

Rows 15–32: Rep Rows 9–14 three more times—58 (66, 72, 80, 86) sts rem.

Row 33: Rep Row 9—56 (64, 70, 78, 84) sts rem.

Work 13 (17, 17, 21, 21, 21) rows even as established, ending with a WS row—piece measures about 5 (5½, 5½, 6, 6)" (12.5 [14, 14, 15, 15] cm) from CO, measured straight up along a single column of sts; do not measure along the curved dart line.

Lace Hem

Legend:

- ☐ k on RS; p on WS
- · k on WS
- ╱ k2tog
- ╲ ssk
- ○ yo
- ⋀ sl 2 sts as if to k2tog, k1, p2sso
- ▢ pattern repeat

Work a lace edging in a lighter weight yarn to give it a more delicate look.

Increase for Waist

Row 1: Knit to marked st, M1, k1 (marked st), M1, work in established patts to end—2 sts inc'd.

Rows 2–8: Work 7 rows even as established.

Rows 9–32: Rep Rows 1–8 three more times—64 (72, 78, 86, 92) sts.

Row 33: Rep Row 1—66 (74, 80, 88, 94) sts.

Cont even as established until piece measures 9½ (10, 10½, 11, 11½)" (24 [25.5, 26.5, 28, 29] cm) from CO, ending with a WS row.

Shape Armhole and Neck

Cont in patt as established, BO 4 (5, 5, 6, 6) sts at beg of next RS row, then BO 3 (3, 4, 4, 4) sts at beg of foll 2 RS rows, then BO 0 (0, 3, 3, 3) sts at beg foll 0 (0, 1, 1, 1) RS row, then BO 2 sts at beg of foll RS row, then BO 1 st at beg of foll 1 (2, 3, 4, 5) RS row(s)—53 (59, 59, 65, 70) sts rem; armhole measures about 1 (1¼, 1¾, 2, 2¼)" (2.5 [3.2, 4.5, 5, 5.5] cm). Work even in patt until armhole measures 1½ (1¾, 2¼, 2½, 2¾)" (3.8 [4.5, 5.5, 6.5, 7] cm), ending with a RS row. Cont in patt, BO 32 (35, 35, 38, 41) sts at beg of next WS row, then BO 8 (9, 9, 10, 11) sts at beg of foll WS row, then BO 5 (6, 6, 6, 7) sts at beg of foll WS row, then BO 2 (2, 2, 3, 3) sts at beg of foll WS row, then BO 1 st at beg of foll 2 (3, 3, 4, 4) WS rows—4 sts rem; armhole measures about 2¾ (3¼, 3¾, 4¼, 4½)" (7 [8.5, 9.5, 11, 11.5] cm). Place sts on holder to be worked later for strap.

FRONT

With MC, CO 27 sts. Purl 1 WS row.

Shape Lower Front Curve

Row 1: (RS) [RT (see Stitch Guide), k3] 5 times, place regular marker on needle (pm), RT, use the backward loop method (see Glossary, page 152) to CO 5 (6, 6, 7, 8) sts—32 (33, 33, 34, 35) sts.

Row 2: Purl to end, pm, CO 5 (6, 6, 7, 8) sts as before—37 (39, 39, 41, 43) sts; 27 marked sts in center. Slip markers (sl m) every row.

Row 3: Knit to marked center sts, [RT, k3] 5 times, RT, knit to end, CO 5 (6, 6, 7, 8) sts—42 (45, 45, 48, 51) sts.

Row 4: Purl to end, CO 5 (6, 6, 7, 8) sts—47 (51, 51, 55, 59) sts.

Rows 5–10: Rep Rows 3 and 4 three more times—77 (87, 87, 97, 107) sts.

Row 11: Knit to marked center sts, work 27 center sts in established patt, knit to end, CO 3 (3, 5, 5, 5) sts—80 (90, 92, 102, 112) sts.

Row 12: Purl to end, CO 3 (3, 5, 5, 5) sts—83 (93, 97, 107, 117) sts.

Rows 13–16: Rep Rows 11 and 12 two more times—95 (105, 117, 127, 137) sts.

Row 17: K2, pm, RT, pm, knit to marked center sts, work 27 center sts in established patt, knit to last 4 sts, pm, RT, pm, k2, CO 4 (5, 5, 6, 7) sts—99 (110, 122, 133, 144) sts; two 2-st groups of RT marked at each side.

Row 18: Purl to end, CO 4 (5, 5, 6, 7) sts—103 (115, 127, 139, 151) sts.

Row 19: Knit to first marked 2-st group, RT, knit to center marked sts, work center 27 sts in established patt, knit to next marked 2-st group, RT, knit to end, CO 5 (6, 7, 8, 9) sts—108 (121, 134, 147, 160) sts.

Row 20: Purl to end, CO 5 (6, 7, 8, 9) sts—113 (127, 141, 155, 169) sts: 27 center sts, 30 (35, 41, 46, 51) St st sts on each side of center, one 2-st RT column outside each St st section (2 RT columns total), 11 (13, 14, 16, 18) St st sts at each end of row; curved lower edge shaping has been completed; piece measures about 2¼" (5.5 cm) from CO at center.

Decrease for Waist

Row 21: K11 (13, 14, 16, 18) to first marked 2-st group, RT, k15 (17, 20, 23, 25), sl 2 tog kwise, k1, p2sso, k12 (15, 18, 20, 23), work 27 center sts in established patt, k12 (15, 18, 20, 23), sl 2 tog kwise, k1, p2sso, k15 (17, 20, 23, 25), RT, k11 (13, 14, 16, 18)—109 (123, 137, 151, 165) sts rem. Place a removable marker in the center st of each double dec just completed to mark dart lines.

Rows 22–26: Work 5 rows even, working RTs as established every RS row.

Row 27: Knit to first marked 2-st group, RT, knit to 1 st before marked dart st, sl 2 tog kwise, k1, p2sso, knit to marked center sts, work center 27 sts in established patt, knit to 1 st before next marked dart st, sl 2 tog kwise, k1,

p2sso, knit to next marked 2-st group, RT, knit to end—105 (119, 133, 147, 161) sts; marked dart st is center st of each double dec.

Rows 28–30: Work 3 rows even as established; piece measures about 3¼" (8.5 cm) from CO at center.

Row 31: Knit to first marked 2-st group, RT, knit to marked center sts, [RT, k3, M1] 2 times, RT, k3, RT, [M1, k3, RT] 2 times, knit to next marked 2-st group, RT, knit to end—109 (123, 137, 151, 165) sts; the 4 outermost 3-st knit columns of the center section have been inc'd to 4 sts each; marked center section now contains 31 sts; work the new sts in St st.

Row 32: Work even as established.

Row 33: Knit to first marked 2-st group, RT, knit to 1 st before marked dart st, sl 2 tog kwise, k1, p2sso, knit to marked center sts, work center 31 sts in established patt, knit to 1 st before next marked dart st, sl 2 tog kwise, k1, p2sso, knit to next marked 2-st group, RT, knit to end—105 (119, 133, 147, 161) sts rem.

Rows 34–38: Work 5 rows even as established.

Rows 39–50: Rep Rows 33–38 two more times—97 (111, 125, 139, 153) sts.

Row 51: Rep Row 33—93 (107, 121, 135, 149) sts rem.

Work 13 (19, 19, 23, 23) rows even as established, ending with a WS row—piece measures 7¼ (7¾, 7¾, 8¼, 8¼)" (18.5 [19.5, 19.5, 21, 21] cm) high at center, and 5 (5½, 5½, 6, 6)" (12.5 [14, 14, 15, 15] cm) high at selvedges.

Increase for Waist

Row 1: Knit to first marked 2-st group, RT, knit to marked center sts, [RT, k4, M1] 2 times, RT, k3, RT, [M1, k4, RT] 2 times, knit to next marked 2-st group, RT, knit to end—97 (111, 125, 139, 153) sts; the 4 outermost 4-st knit columns of the center section have been inc'd to 5 sts each; marked center section now contains 35 sts; work the new sts in St st.

Row 2: Work even.

Row 3: Knit to first marked 2-st group, RT, knit to marked dart st, M1, k1 (dart st), M1, knit to marked center sts, work center 35 sts in established patt, knit to next marked dart st, M1, k1 (dart st), M1, knit to next marked 2-st group, RT, knit to end—101 (115, 129, 143, 157) sts.

Rows 4–10: Work 7 rows even as established.

Rows 11–26: Rep Rows 3–10 two more times—109 (123, 137, 151, 165) sts.

Row 27: Rep Row 3—113 (127, 141, 155, 169) sts.

Rows 28–32: Work 5 rows even as established.

Row 33: Knit to first marked 2-st group, RT, knit to marked center sts, [RT, k5, M1] 2 times, RT, k3, RT, [M1, k5, RT] 2 times, knit to next marked 2-st group, RT, knit to end—117 (131, 145, 159, 173) sts; the 4 outermost 5-st knit columns of the center section have been inc'd to 6 sts each; marked center section now contains 39 sts; work the new sts in St st.

Row 34: Work even.

Row 35: Knit to first marked 2-st group, RT, knit to marked dart st, M1, k1 (dart st), M1, knit to marked center sts, work center 39 sts in established patt, knit to next marked dart st, M1, k1 (dart st), M1, knit to next marked 2-st group, RT, knit to end—121 (135, 149, 163, 177) sts.

Work 1 (5, 9, 11, 13) row(s) even, ending with a WS row—piece measures 11¼ (12¼, 12¾, 13¼, 13¾)" (28.5 [31, 32.5, 33.5, 35] cm) from CO at center, and 9 (10, 10½, 11, 11½)" (23 [25.5, 26.5, 28, 29] cm) at selvedges.

Shape Front Neck and Armhole

Left front: *Notes:* When working short-rows to shape front neck, cont to work all RT sts as established every RS row. For each short-row, simply turn the work and do not wrap the sts at the turning points; the small holes left at the turning points will be covered by the lace yoke trim.

Short-row 1: (RS) Work as established to marked center sts, work next 10 sts in patt, pm on needle to indicate beg of center front neck, turn—51 (58, 65, 72, 79) sts just worked for left front; 70 (77, 84, 91, 98) sts unworked at end of row to be worked later for center front and right front neck and armhole.

Even-numbered Short-rows 2–16: (WS) Purl to end.

Short-rows 3, 5, and 7: Work to 6 (7, 7, 8, 9) sts before previous turning point, turn.

Short-row 9: BO 4 (5, 5, 6, 6) sts at armhole edge (beg of RS rows), work to 6 (7, 7, 8, 9) sts before previous turning point, turn.

Short-row 11: BO 3 (4, 5, 5, 5) sts, work to 4 (4, 5, 6, 6) sts before previous turning point, turn.

Short-row 13: BO 2 (3, 4, 4, 5) sts, work to 4 (4, 5, 6, 6) before previous turning point, turn.

Short-row 15: BO 2 (2, 3, 3, 4) sts, work to 3 (3, 4, 4, 5) sts before previous turning point, turn.

Short-row 17: BO 1 (1, 2, 2, 2) st(s), work 1 st (2 sts before previous turning point), turn—12 (15, 19, 20, 22) sts total BO at armhole.

Short-row 18: P2, turn—armhole measures about 1¼" (3.2 cm).

Next row: (RS) Work in patt to m at beg of center front sts, remove m, work 19 sts in patt, pm on needle for beg of right front sts, work in patt to end—51 (58, 65, 72, 79) sts for right front.

Right front:

Short-row 1: (WS) Purl to 6 sts before right front m, turn.

Even-numbered Short-rows 2–16: (RS) Work in patt to end.

Short-rows 3, 5, and 7: Purl to 6 (7, 7, 8, 9) sts before previous turning point, turn.

Short-row 9: BO 4 (5, 5, 6, 6) sts at armhole edge (beg of WS rows), purl to 6 (7, 7, 8, 9) sts before previous turning point, turn.

Short-row 11: BO 3 (4, 5, 5, 5) sts, purl to 4 (4, 5, 6, 6) sts before previous turning point, turn.

Short-row 13: BO 2 (3, 4, 4, 5) sts, purl to 4 (4, 5, 6, 6) sts before previous turning point, turn.

Short-row 15: BO 2 (2, 3, 3, 4) sts, purl to 3 (3, 4, 4, 5) sts before previous turning point, turn.

Short-row 17: BO 1 (1, 2, 2, 2) st(s), p1 (2 sts before previous turning point), turn—12 (15, 19, 20, 22) sts total BO at armhole.

Short-row 18: Work to end in patt, turn—armhole measures about 1¼" (3.2 cm); 97 (105, 111, 123, 133) sts total.

Lace Yoke

Removing markers as you come to them, knit 1 WS row across all sts, dec 0 (2, 2, 2, 0) sts evenly spaced as you go—97 (103, 109, 121, 133) sts rem.

Row 1: (RS) K6, *yo, ssk, k4; rep from * to last st, k1.

Rows 2–4: Work even in St st.

Row 5: K3, *yo, ssk, k4; rep from * to last 4 sts, yo, ssk, k2.

Row 6–8: Work even in St st.

Rows 9–12: Rep Rows 1–4 once more—armholes measure about 2½" (6.5 cm).

Mark center 69 (75, 81, 93, 105) sts for center front neck. *Next row:* (RS) Work in patt to marked center sts, join new yarn and BO center 69 (75, 81, 93, 105) sts, work in patt to end—14 sts at each side. Working each side separately, at each neck edge BO 4 sts once, then BO 3 sts once, then BO 2 sts once, then BO 1 st once—4 sts rem each side; front armholes measure about 3¾" (9.5 cm). Working 4-st straps separately, work even in St st until straps measure 9½ (10, 9½, 10, 10¾)" (24 [25.5, 24, 25.5, 27.5] cm). *Note:* These straps lengths will produce armholes about 8 (8½, 8½, 9, 9½)" (20.5 [21.5, 21.5, 23, 24] cm) high; instructions are given below in Finishing for customizing strap length. Place straps sts on holders.

FINISHING

Block pieces to measurements. With MC threaded on a tapestry needle, sew backs to front along side seams. Pin live sts at ends of straps tog temporarily. Try on corset, and adjust length of straps, adding or removing rows as necessary to achieve the best fit. With yarn threaded on a tapestry needle, use the Kitchener st (see Glossary, page 155) to join 4 live sts of each front and back strap tog, being careful not to twist straps.

Buttonhole Band

With MC, RS facing, and beg at lower edge of left back, pick up and knit 78 (86, 90, 98, 102) sts along straight edge of back opening.

Row 1: (WS) P4, *k1, p3; rep from *, to last 2 sts, k1, p1.

Row 2: (RS) K1, p1, *k1, yo, ssk, p1; rep from *, to last 4 sts, k1, yo, ssk, k1—19 (21, 22, 24, 25) yo buttonholes completed.

Row 3: Rep Row 1.

BO all sts.

Lace Hem

With MC, RS facing, and beg at lower edge of right back opening, pick up and knit 227 (254, 281, 317, 344) sts evenly spaced around entire lower edge of body. Knit 3 rows, ending with a WS row. Change to CC. *Next row:* (RS) K2, yo, *k3, yo; rep from * to last 3 sts, k3—302 (338, 374, 422, 458) sts. Knit 1 WS row. Work Rows 1–10 of Lace Hem chart (see page 34). BO all sts.

Neckline Trim for Drawstring

With MC, RS facing, and beg at left back neck opening, pick up and knit 302 (326, 326, 358, 390) sts along left back neck, inner edge of left strap, front neck, inner edge of right strap, and back right back neck, ending at right back neck opening. Knit 1 WS row for garter ridge, then knit 1 RS row. *Next row:* (WS) P2, *yo, p2tog, p2; rep from * to end. Knit 2 rows for garter ridge. BO all sts.

Lace Yoke Trim

With CC and RS facing, pick up and knit 97 (103, 109, 121, 133) sts just below the garter st ridge at base of lace yoke section.

Rows 1 and 3: (WS) Purl.

Row 2: (RS) K2, *yo, ssk; rep from * to last st, k1.

BO as foll: *BO 2 sts, [return st on right needle to left needle and knit this st again] 3 times; rep from * to end, BO last 3 sts.

I-Cord Drawstring

With MC, CO 3 sts. Work I-cord (see Glossary, page 155) until piece measures about 65 (69, 73, 77, 81)" (165 [175.5, 185.5, 195.5, 205.5] cm) from CO. BO all sts. Beg and ending at back opening, thread I-cord through holes in neckline trim.

Weave in loose ends. Block lightly again, if desired. Sew buttons to right back underneath buttonholes of left back, with a button opposite every buttonhole eyelet or every other eyelet as desired.

Lace doesn't have to be fussy to be beautiful.

FEATHERLIGHT LINGERIE DRESS
MARI LYNN PATRICK

We're all familiar with gossamer shawls, but **Mari Lynn Patrick** went a step further and created a featherweight dress with handkerchief hem. She combined a fine mohair/silk yarn with relatively large needles to knit up a cloud-like fabric with lace accents. The skirt is worked first in two halves joined at the center to form a rectangle with a hole in the center. The bodice is worked next with a diminutive lace motif. The bodice and skirt are then sewn together with elastic thread. Additional bands of lace at the neck and hem add to the fine-lingerie look.

STITCH GUIDE

Fleurette Lace: *Note:* The pattern begins as a multiple of 6 sts plus 5, increases to a multiple of 8 sts plus 5 after completing Rows 3 and 9, then decreases back to a multiple of 6 sts plus 5 after completing Rows 5 and 11.
Row 1: (RS) K2, *k1, yo, ssk, k1, k2tog, yo; rep from * to last 3 sts, k3.
Even-numbered Rows 2–10: Purl.
Row 3: K4, *yo, k3; rep from * to last st, k1—patt is now a multiple of 8 sts plus 5.
Row 5: K2, k2tog, *yo, ssk, k1, k2tog, yo, sl 2 tog kwise, k1, p2sso; rep from * to last 9 sts, yo, ssk, k1, k2tog, yo, ssk, k2—patt is now a multiple of 6 sts plus 5.
Row 7: K2, *k1, k2tog, yo, k1, yo, ssk; rep from * to last 3 sts, k3.
Row 9: Rep Row 3—patt is now a multiple of 8 sts plus 5.
Row 11: K2, *k1, k2tog, yo, sl 2 tog kwise, k1, p2sso, yo, ssk; rep from * to last 3 sts, k3—patt is now a multiple of 6 sts plus 5.
Row 12: Purl.
Repeat Rows 1–12 for pattern.

SKIRT

First Half

With single strand of yarn and largest straight needles, CO 126 (136, 144, 154, 162) sts. Knit 1 RS row. Cont in St st, and beg with the next WS row, use the cable method (see Glossary, page 152) to CO 2 sts at the beg next 14 rows—154 (164, 172, 182, 190) sts; piece measures about 2½" (6.5 cm) from CO. Cont even in St st until piece measures 10 (10½, 11, 11, 11½)" (25.5 [26.5, 28, 28, 29] cm) from CO, ending with a WS row.

FINISHED SIZE
30 (34, 38, 42, 46)" [76 [86.5, 96.5, 106.5, 117] cm) bust circumference. Dress shown measures 30" (76 cm).

YARN
Sportweight (CYCA #2 Fine).
Shown here: Rowan Kidsilk Haze (70% kid mohair, 30% silk; 229 yd [209 m]/25 g): #590 pearl, 4 (5, 5, 6, 6) balls.

NEEDLES
Skirt and bodice back—size 8 (5 mm): straight. Bodice front and sides—size 3 (3.25 mm): straight. Lace hem—size 7 (4.5 mm): 40" (100 cm) circular (cir). Waist ribbing—size 7 (4.5 mm): 24" (60 cm) circular (cir). Adjust needle size if necessary to obtain the correct gauge. *Note:* Bamboo or other lightweight needles work best with this fine yarn.

NOTIONS
Stitch holders; removable markers or waste yarn; tapestry needle; 1 spool of elastic thread in matching color (available at fabric stores).

GAUGE
18 stitches and 23 rows = 4" (10 cm) in stockinette stitch with a single strand of yarn on larger straight needles. 20½ stitches and 37 rows = 4" (10 cm) in fleurette lace pattern after blocking with a single strand of yarn on smaller straight needles.

Shape waist opening: With RS facing, k69 (71, 73, 75, 75), join a second ball of yarn and BO center 16 (22, 26, 32, 40) sts, knit to end—69 (71, 73, 75, 75) sts each side. Working each side separately, BO at each waist opening edge 2 sts 6 times, then BO 1 st 5 times—52 (54, 56, 58, 58) sts rem each side; piece measures about 13¾ (14¼, 14¾, 14¾, 15¼)" (35 [36, 37.5, 37.5, 38.5] cm) from CO. Place sts on holders.

Second Half

Make the second half the same as the first.

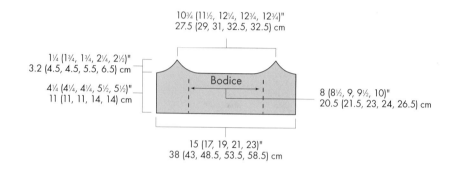

10¾ (11½, 12¼, 12¾, 12¾)"
27.5 (29, 31, 32.5, 32.5) cm

1¼ (1¾, 1¾, 2¼, 2½)"
3.2 (4.5, 4.5, 5.5, 6.5) cm

Bodice

4¼ (4¼, 4¼, 5½, 5½)"
11 (11, 11, 14, 14) cm

8 (8½, 9, 9½, 10)"
20.5 (21.5, 23, 24, 26.5) cm

15 (17, 19, 21, 23)"
38 (43, 48.5, 53.5, 58.5) cm

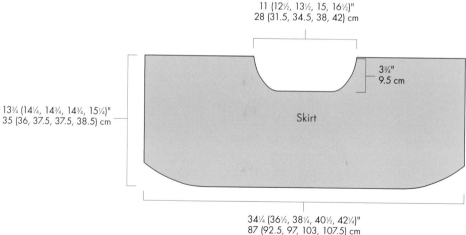

11 (12½, 13½, 15, 16½)"
28 (31.5, 34.5, 38, 42) cm

3¾"
9.5 cm

Skirt

13¾ (14¼, 14¾, 14¾, 15¼)"
35 (36, 37.5, 37.5, 38.5) cm

34¼ (36½, 38¼, 40½, 42¼)"
87 (92.5, 97, 103, 107.5) cm

Join Halves

Place 52 (54, 56, 58, 58) held sts from each half on smaller straight needles and hold needles with WS facing tog. Using the largest-size straight needle and the three-needle method (see Glossary, page 151) loosely BO sts tog. Join sts on other side of waist opening in the same manner.

Hem

With double strand of yarn, longer cir needle, RS facing, and beg at the join between the skirt halves, pick up and knit 40 (43, 44, 44, 45) sts along straight selvedge of skirt, 17 sts along curved edge, 111 (121, 127, 135, 141) sts across CO edge, 17 sts along other curved edge, and 40 (43, 44, 44, 45) sts along other straight selvedge, ending at other join—225 (241, 249, 257, 265) sts total. Purl 1 WS row. Work lace patt for skirt hem as foll:

The soft halo of mohair/silk yarn adds a romantic touch to simple lace motifs.

Row 1: *K1, yo, ssk, k3, k2tog, yo; rep from * to last st, k1.

Rows 2 and 4: (WS) Purl.

Row 3: *K2, yo, ssk, k1, k2tog, yo, k1; rep from * to last st, k1.

Row 5: Purl 1 RS row.

BO all sts kwise on next WS row. Work hem for second half of skirt in the same manner. With yarn threaded on a tapestry needle, sew selvedges of lace hems tog.

BODICE

Front-and-Sides Piece

With single strand of yarn and smallest straight needles, CO 113 (131, 149, 167, 185) sts. Purl 1 WS row. Rep Rows 1–12 of fleurette patt (see Stitch Guide) 3 (3, 3, 4, 4) times, ending with Row 12 of patt. Work even in St st for 2 rows, ending with a WS row—piece measures about 4¼ (4¼, 4¼, 5½, 5½)" (11 [11, 11, 14, 14] cm) from CO.

Shape front neck and armholes: Mark center 29 (33, 37, 39, 39) sts for front neck. *Next row:* (RS) BO 15 (17, 19, 21, 23) sts, knit to marked center sts, join a second ball of yarn and BO 29 (33, 37, 39, 39) sts for front neck, knit to end. *Next row:* (WS) BO 15 (17, 19, 21, 23) sts at beg of first group of sts, purl to end of first group, purl across second group of sts—27 (32, 37, 43, 50) sts at each side. *Note:* The neck and armhole shaping are worked at the same time; read all the way through the next section before continuing. Cont in St st and working each side separately, at each neck edge BO 3 sts 3 times, then BO 2 sts 2 times, and *at the same time,* at each end of row (armhole edges), BO 4 sts 0 (0, 3, 4, 5) times, then BO 3 sts 3 (4, 3, 3, 4) times, then BO 2 sts 2 (3, 1, 2, 2) time(s)—1 st rem at each side. Mark each rem st as a "peak" for the bodice front. Fasten off each peak st.

Center Back Panel

With double strand of yarn, largest straight needles, and RS facing, pick up and knit 23 (23, 23, 29, 29) sts along one straight selvedge of front-and-sides piece. Beg and end with k1, work in k1, p1 rib until piece measures 8 (8½, 9, 9½, 10)" (20.5 [21.5, 23, 24, 25.5] cm) from pick-up row. BO all sts. With double strand of yarn threaded on a tapestry needle, sew BO edge of center back panel to other selvedge of front-and-sides piece to join the bodice into a cylinder—bodice measures about 30 (34, 38, 42, 46)" (76 [86.5, 96.5, 106.5, 117] cm) around.

Back and Armhole Trim

With double strand of yarn, largest straight needles, RS facing, and beg at right front peak, pick up and knit 30 (35, 41, 46, 50) sts along shaped edge of right armhole, 37 (39, 41, 43, 47) sts across top edge of center back panel, and 30 (35, 41, 46, 50) sts along shaped edge of left armhole, ending at left front peak—97 (109, 123, 135, 147) sts total.

Worked on large needles, even stockinette stitch can have a lacy look.

Row 1: (WS) K1, *p1, k1; rep from * to end.

Row 2: (RS) P1, *k1, p1; rep from * to end.

Rep Rows 1 and 2 once more. BO all sts.

Front Neck Trim and Straps

With double strand of yarn, largest straight needles, RS facing, and beg at left front peak, pick up and knit 49 (53, 55, 59, 59) sts evenly spaced along front neck edge, ending at right front peak. Cont as foll:

Row 1: (WS) P1, *k1, p1; rep from * to end.

Row 2: (RS) [K1, p1] 2 times, sl 1 kwise, k2tog, psso, work in established rib to last 7 sts, sl 1 kwise, k2tog, psso, work in established rib to end—45 (49, 51, 55, 55) sts rem.

Work even established rib for 2 more rows. *Next row:* (WS) Work 5 sts in established rib, join a second ball of yarn and BO center 35 (39, 41, 45, 45) sts, work in rib to end—5 sts rem at each side for straps. Working each side separately, cont in rib as established until straps measure 12 (12, 12½, 12½, 13)" (30.5 [30.5, 31.5, 31.5, 33] cm). Place sts on holders. With yarn threaded on a tapestry needle, sew selvedges of front neck trim to armhole trim at each side.

FINISHING

Block pieces to measurements, being careful not to flatten the mohair halo.

Waist Ribbing

With double strand of yarn, shorter cir needle, and RS facing, pick up and knit 116 (132, 146, 154, 168) sts around entire lower edge of bodice. Pm, and join for working in the rnd. Work in k1, p1 rib for 4 rnds. BO all sts loosely in rib.

Join Bodice to Skirt

Pin BO edge of waist ribbing to waist opening in skirt, being careful to align the centers of the front and back bodice with center front and back of skirt. Using a double strand of elastic thread on a tapestry needle, carefully sew the waist ribbing into the skirt opening, easing in any fullness.

Attach Straps

Pin ends of straps temporarily to upper edge of center back panel close to where back panel joins the lace patt, with ends of straps touching the pick-up row for the back and armhole trim so rib trim overlaps straps. Mark positions where best fit for straps is achieved, making sure the straps are place symmetrically. Adjust length of straps, adding or removing rows as necessary to achieve the best fit, then BO ends of straps. Sew straps to marked positions, first along the pick-up row of back and armhole trim, then across the BO edge of back and armhole trim. Weave in loose ends.

LITTLE SILK SHRUG
PAM ALLEN

A lace garment doesn't get much simpler than this little shrug. The lace motif has a four-row repeat—and two of those four rows are simple purl rows—that is easily memorized. The shrug is worked as a plain rectangle of lace that is bordered with garter stitch to give a casual and elastic finish to the edges. Because there's no shaping and the stitch pattern is easy, this is a great project for first-time lace knitters. A delicious handdyed silk yarn is a good foil for the shrug's simple shape and repeating stitch pattern.

STITCH GUIDE

Miniature Leaf Pattern: (multiple of 6 sts + 4)
Row 1: (RS) K2, *k3, yo, sl 1, k2tog, psso, yo; rep from * to last 2 sts, k2.
Rows 2 and 4: (WS) Purl.
Row 3: K2, *yo, sl 1, k2tog, psso, yo, k3; rep from * to last 2 sts, k2.
Repeat Rows 1–4 for pattern.

FINISHED SIZE
About 26" (66 cm) long from cuff to cuff, 10½" (26.5 cm) circumference at cuff, and 11" (28 cm) long at center back including edging.

YARN
Worsted weight (CYCA #4 Medium).
Shown here: La Lana Phat Silk Fine (50% silk, 50% wool; 142 yd [130 m]/2 oz): pale indigo, 2 skeins.

NEEDLES
Sizes 7 (4.5 mm) and 8 (5 mm): straight. Edging—size 7 (4.5 mm): 24" (60 cm) circular (cir). Adjust needle size if necessary to obtain the correct gauge.

NOTIONS
Markers (m); tapestry needle.

GAUGE
18 stitches and 28 rows = 4" (10 cm) in stockinette stitch on larger needles; 17½ stitches and 26 rows = 4" (10 cm) in miniature leaf pattern on larger needles.

SHRUG

With smaller straight needles and using the long-tail method (see Glossary, page 153), CO 46 sts. Knit 5 rows, beg and ending with a RS row. Change to larger needles. *Next row:* (WS) Purl. Rep Rows 1–4 of miniature leaf patt (see Stitch Guide) until piece measures 25½" (65 cm) from CO, ending with a RS row. Change to smaller needles. Knit 4 rows, ending with a RS row. With WS facing, BO all sts knitwise.

FINISHING

Fold shrug in half lengthwise. With yarn threaded on a tapestry needle, sew the selvedges tog for 2" (5 cm) at each short end, beg at the CO or BO edge and sewing toward the center.

Edging

Note: The exact number of sts picked up for the edging is not critical and may vary depending on individual row gauge; it is more important to pick up 2 sts for every 3 rows evenly all the way around the

Choose a project
that has no shaping
for your first venture
into lace knitting.

opening. Join yarn to center of one long side of opening. With cir needle and RS facing, *pick up and knit 1 st in each of next 2 selvedge sts, skip 1 selvedge st*; rep from * to * to side seam, place marker (pm), rep from * to * across second long side to other seam, pm, rep from * to * to starting point at center of first long side, pm, and join for working in the rnd—about 180–192 sts. *Next rnd:* *Purl to 2 sts before seam marker, p2tog, slip marker (sl m), p2togtbl (see Glossary, page 154); rep from * once more, purl to end of rnd—4 sts dec'd. *Next rnd:* *Knit to 2 sts before seam marker, k2tog, sl m, ssk; rep from * once more, knit to end of rnd— 4 sts dec'd. *Next rnd:* *BO all sts purlwise to 2 sts before marker, p2tog, BO 1, remove m, p2togtbl, BO 1 st; rep from * once more, BO rem sts.

Weave in loose ends. Block lightly if desired.

A little bit of lace will dress up any outfit.

THE ESSENTIAL TANK TOP
LAURA ZUKAITE

A large-scale lace motif worked in fine yarn on large needles creates an appealing airy fabric in **Laura Zukaite's** lace tank. Worked from the bottom up in two simple pieces with minimal edging, this tank shows off the rounded lines of the lace pattern beautifully. The front and back are joined by tiny chains of stitches at the shoulders. Wear the tank belted or let it hang straight; wear it with jeans or a flowy dress—whatever you do, you can't go wrong.

NOTES

❖ Work with two strands of yarn held together unless otherwise noted.

❖ For selvedge stitches, slip the first stitch of every row as if to purl with yarn in back and knit the last stitch of every row. The selvedge stitches are not shown on the charts.

❖ Work armhole decreases inside selvedge stitches as follows: On right-side (RS) rows, sl 1 (selvedge st), ssk, work in pattern to last 3 sts, k2tog, k1 (selvedge st); on wrong-side (WS) rows, sl 1, p2tog, purl to last 3 sts, ssp (see Glossary, page 154), k1.

❖ When shaping the armholes, if there are not enough stitches to work a yarnover and its companion decrease, work the stitches in stockinette instead. If there are enough stitches to work only one of the two yarnovers associated with a double decrease, substitute a single decrease (either k2tog or ssk) for the double decrease and work the single yarnover in its usual place in the pattern.

FINISHED SIZE
34 (39½, 45, 50½)" (86.5 [100.5, 114.5, 128.5] cm) bust/chest circumference. Tank shown measures 34" (86.5 cm).

YARN
Fingering weight (CYCA #1 Super Fine).
Shown here: Alpaca with a Twist Fino (70% baby alpaca, 30% silk; 875 yd [800 m]/50 g): #1001 duchesse blue, 3 (4, 4, 5) skeins (used double).

NEEDLES
Size 6 (4 mm). Adjust needle size if necessary to obtain the correct gauge.

NOTIONS
Markers (m); tapestry needle; size G/6 (4.25 mm) crochet hook

GAUGE
20½ sts and 30½ rows = 4" (10 cm) in pattern from Large Lace Petal chart with yarn doubled, after blocking.

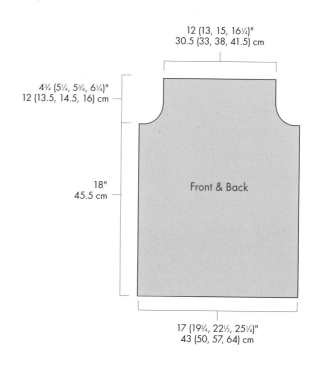

12 (13, 15, 16¼)"
30.5 (33, 38, 41.5) cm

4¾ (5¼, 5¾, 6¼)"
12 (13.5, 14.5, 16) cm

18"
45.5 cm

Front & Back

17 (19¾, 22½, 25¼)"
43 (50, 57, 64) cm

BACK

With yarn doubled, CO 87 (101, 115, 129) sts. Slipping the first st and knitting the last st of every row for selvedges (see Notes), work the center 85 (99, 113, 127) sts according to Rows 1–36 of Large Lace Petal chart a total of 3 times, then work Rows 1–6 once more—114 rows total. Change to Small Lace Petal chart and work Rows 1–24 once—138 pattern rows total; piece measures about 18" (45.5 cm) from CO for all sizes.

Shape Armholes

Cont in patt, BO 6 (7, 8, 9) sts at beg of next 2 rows, then BO 4 (5, 5, 6) sts at beg of next 2 rows (see Notes)—67 (77, 89, 99) sts rem. Dec 1 st each end of needle on next 2 rows (see Notes), then dec 1 st at each end of needle on foll 1 (3, 4, 6) RS row(s)—61 (67, 77, 83) sts rem. Work even in patt until armholes measure 4¾ (5¼, 5¾, 6¼)" (12 [13.5, 14.5, 16] cm), ending with Row 12 (16, 20, 24) of Small Lace Petal chart. BO all sts.

FRONT

Work as for back until Rows 1–36 of Large Lace Petal chart have been worked a total of 3 times, then work Rows 1–30 once more—138 rows total; piece measures about 18" (45.5 cm) from CO for all sizes.

Small Lace Petal

(chart rows, right-hand labels, odd numbers 1–23)

23
21
19
17
15
13
11
9
7
5
3
1

Small Lace Petal

(chart rows, right-hand labels, odd numbers 1–35)

35
33
31
29
27
25
23
21
19
17
15
13
11
9
7
5
3
1

□	k on RS; p on WS	╱	k2tog	⋏	sl 1 kwise, k2tog, psso
○	yo	╲	ssk	☐	pattern repeat

Shape Armholes

Cont in patt, BO 6 (7, 8, 9) sts at beg of next 2 rows, then BO 4 (5, 5, 6) sts at beg of next 2 rows—67 (77, 89, 99) sts. Dec 1 st each end of needle on next 2 rows, then dec 1 st each end of needle on foll 1 (3, 3, 3) RS row(s), then work 5 (1, 1, 1) row(s) even, ending with Row 6 of Large Lace Petal chart—61 (67, 79, 89) sts; armhole is 12 patt rows high. Change to Small Lace Petal chart and establish patt for your size as foll:

Size 34" only: Sl 1 (selvedge st), k1, work Row 1 of chart over center 57 sts, k1, k1 (selvedge st).

Size 39½" only: Sl 1 (selvedge st), k4, work the 14-st patt rep of Row 1 indicated by the red outline 4 times, k5, k1 (selvedge st).

Size 45" only: Sl 1 (selvedge st), ssk, k1, work the 14-st patt rep of Row 1 indicated by the red outline 5 times, k2, k2tog, k1 (selvedge st)—77 sts.

Size 50½" only: Sl 1 (selvedge st), k1, work the 14-st patt rep of Row 1 indicated by the red outline 6 times, k2, k1 (selvedge st). Cont in patt, dec 1 st each end of needle on Rows 3, 5, and 7 of chart—83 sts.

Lace—the perfect accessory.

All sizes: Work even in patt until armholes measure 4¾ (5¼, 5¾, 6¼)" (12 [13.5, 14.5, 16] cm), ending with Row 24 (4, 8, 12) of Small Lace Petal chart. BO all sts.

FINISHING

Block to measurements. With yarn threaded on a tapestry needle, sew side seams.

Armhole Edgings and Straps

With crochet hook, 4 strands of yarn held tog, and beg at right side seam, work a row of sc (see Glossary, page 154, for crochet instructions) evenly along right back armhole to BO edge, then work a crochet chain about 2 (4, 6, 6½") (5 [10, 15, 16.5] cm) long. Temporarily pin the end of the crochet chain to the top right front corner, and try on the tank to check strap length. Increase or decrease the length of the crochet chain to achieve the best fit, and note the number of chain sts so you can work the second strap to match. Being careful not to twist the chain, work a row of sc evenly along right front armhole edge, and end by joining to the first sc at side seam with a sl st. Fasten off last st. Work left armhole edging and strap in the same manner.

Weave in loose ends.

A longtime fan of the traditional feather and fan stitch pattern, **Pam Allen** worked it on a grand scale for this classic jacket. The structure of this lace pattern—groups of yarnovers alternating with groups of decreases—creates decorative scallops that are preserved in the cast-on edges. To keep this project simple, Pam added very little shaping (the roll-over collar is simply an extension of the fronts) and worked the sleeve increases in panels of stockinette stitch that border the lace motif.

BACK

With smaller needles and using the long-tail method (see Glossary, page 153), CO 66 (72 (78, 91, 97) sts. Knit 4 rows. Change to larger needles.

Row 1: (RS) Knit.

Row 2: Purl.

Row 3: K2, [k2tog] 2 (3, 4, 2, 3) times, [yo, k1] 2 (3, 4, 2, 3) times, place marker (pm), work center 50 (50, 50, 75, 75) sts for feather and fan patt as *[yo, k1] 4 times, [ssk] 4 times, k1, [k2tog] 4 times, [yo, k1] 4 times, pm; rep from * 1 (1, 1, 2, 2) more time(s), [yo, k1] 2 (3, 4, 2, 3) times, [ssk] 2 (3, 4, 2, 3) times, k2—2 (2, 2, 3, 3) marked full 25-st reps of feather and fan patt at center, 6 (9, 12, 6, 9) sts for partial patt rep on each side of main patt, 2 edge sts at each end of needle.

Row 4: Knit.

Cont in patt until Rows 1–4 have been worked a total of 20 times, ending with Row 4—80 patt rows total; piece measures 17" (43 cm) from CO for all sizes, measured straight up along a single column of sts at center back.

Shape Armholes

Note: When working armhole shaping, discontinue the partial patt rep at each side; instead, work the partial rep sts and edge sts as St st on patt Rows 1–3, and knit them on patt Row 4 to form a garter ridge to match the feather and fan patt. BO 4 (4, 5, 5, 7) sts at beg of next 2 rows (Rows 1 and 2 of patt)—58 (64, 68, 81, 83) sts rem; 4 (7, 9, 3, 4) sts on each side of marked full patt reps at center. Cont as established, dec 1 st each end of needle every RS row

FINISHED SIZE

33 (36, 39, 45½, 48½)" (84 [91.5, 99, 115.5, 123] cm) bust/chest circumference with center front edges overlapping about 1" (2.5 cm). Sweater shown measures 33" (84 cm).

YARN

Chunky weight (CYCA #5 Bulky).

Shown here: Tahki Kerry (50% wool, 50% alpaca; 90 yd [82 m]/50 g): #5009 green, 9 (10, 11, 12, 14) balls.

NEEDLES

Body and sleeves—size 10½ (6.5 mm): straight. Edging—size 10 (6 mm): straight. Adjust needle size if necessary to obtain the correct gauge.

NOTIONS

Markers (m); stitch holders; tapestry needle.

GAUGE

14½ stitches and 19 rows = 4" (10 cm) in stockinette stitch with garter ridges using larger needles; 25 stitches (1 pattern repeat) = 6¼" (16 cm) and 19 rows = 4" (10 cm) in feather and fan pattern using larger needles, after slightly stretching, blocking, steaming, and being allowed to relax.

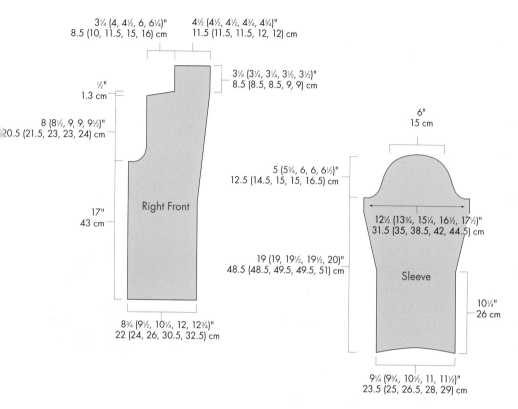

3¼ (4, 4½, 6, 6¼)"
8.5 (10, 11.5, 15, 16) cm

4½ (4½, 4½, 4¾, 4¾)"
11.5 (11.5, 11.5, 12, 12) cm

3¼ (3¼, 3¼, 3½, 3½)"
8.5 (8.5, 8.5, 9, 9) cm

½"
1.3 cm

8 (8½, 9, 9, 9½)"
20.5 (21.5, 23, 23, 24) cm

Right Front

17"
43 cm

8¾ (9½, 10¼, 12, 12¾)"
22 (24, 26, 30.5, 32.5) cm

6"
15 cm

5 (5¾, 6, 6, 6½)"
12.5 (14.5, 15, 15, 16.5) cm

12½ (13¾, 15¼, 16½, 17½)"
31.5 (35, 38.5, 42, 44.5) cm

19 (19, 19½, 19½, 20)"
48.5 (48.5, 49.5, 49.5, 51) cm

Sleeve

10¼"
26 cm

9¼ (9¾, 10½, 11, 11½)"
23.5 (25, 26.5, 28, 29) cm

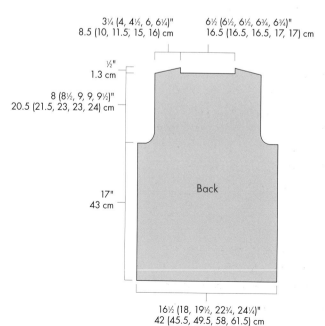

3¼ (4, 4½, 6, 6¼)"
8.5 (10, 11.5, 15, 16) cm

6½ (6½, 6½, 6¾, 6¾)"
16.5 (16.5, 16.5, 17, 17) cm

½"
1.3 cm

8 (8½, 9, 9, 9½)"
20.5 (21.5, 23, 23, 24) cm

Back

17"
43 cm

16½ (18, 19½, 22¾, 24¼)"
42 (45.5, 49.5, 58, 61.5) cm

3 times, ending with Row 3 of patt—52
(58, 62, 75, 77) sts rem; 1 (4, 6, 0, 1)
st(s) on each side of marked full patt reps
at center. Work 3 rows even, ending
with Row 2 of patt. Reestablish patt on
next row as foll: (RS, Row 3 of patt) K1
(1, 0, 0, 1) for edge st, k2tog 0 (1, 2,
0, 0) time(s), [yo, k1] 0 (1, 2, 0, 0) time(s),
work center 50 (50, 50, 75, 75) sts for
feather and fan patt as *[yo, k1] 4 times,
[ssk] 4 times, k1, [k2tog] 4 times, [yo, k1]
4 times; rep from * 1 (1, 1, 2, 2) more
time(s), [yo, k1] 0 (1, 2, 0, 0) time(s), [ssk]
0 (1, 2, 0, 0) time(s), k1 (1, 0, 0, 1) edge
st—2 (2, 2, 3, 3) marked full 25-st reps
of feather and fan patt at center, 0 (3, 6,
0, 0) sts for partial patt rep on each side
of main patt, 1 (1, 0, 0, 1) edge st(s) at
each end of needle. Cont as established,
until armholes measure about 8 (8½, 9, 9,
9½)" (20.5 [21.5, 23, 23, 24] cm), ending with Row 2 of patt.

Shape Shoulders and Back Neck
Work short-rows (see Glossary, page
156) as foll:
Short-row 1: (RS) K13 (16, 18, 24, 25),
   BO center 26 (26, 26, 27, 27) sts, k7
   (8, 9, 12, 13), wrap next st, turn.
Short-row 2: (WS) K7 (8, 9, 12, 13), turn.
Short-row 3: K13 (16, 18, 24, 25) to
   end, working the wrapped st tog with
   its wrap.
Place the last 13 (16, 18, 24, 25) sts just
worked on holder for left back shoulder.
With WS facing, join yarn to sts for right
shoulder at neck edge.
Short-row 1: (WS) K7 (8, 9, 12, 13),
   wrap next st, turn.

Short-row 2: (RS) K7 (8, 9, 12, 13), turn.

Short-row 3: P13 (16, 18, 24, 25) to end, working the wrapped st tog with its wrap.

Place sts on holder for right back shoulder.

RIGHT FRONT

With smaller needles, CO 35 (38, 41, 48, 51) sts. Knit 4 rows. Change to larger needles.

Row 1: (RS) Knit.

Row 2: Purl to last 2 sts, k2 (center front sts; work in garter st).

Row 3: Establish patt for your size as foll:

Sizes 33 (36, 39)" only: K2 (center front sts), pm, work next 25 sts for feather and fan patt as [yo, k1] 4 times, [ssk] 4 times, k1, [k2tog] 4 times, [yo, k1] 4 times, pm, [yo, k1] 2 (3, 4) times, [ssk] 2 (3, 4) times, k2—2 sts at center front edge, 1 marked full 25-st rep of feather and fan patt, 6 (9, 12) sts for partial patt rep, 2 edge sts at side seam edge.

Sizes (45½, 48½)" only: K2 (center front sts), pm, work next 25 sts for feather and fan patt as [yo, k1] 4 times, [ssk] 4 times, k1, [k2tog] 4 times, [yo, k1] 4 times, pm, work next (19, 22) sts for partial patt as [yo, k1] (2, 3) times, [ssk] (2, 3) times, k1, [k2tog] 2 times, [yo, k1] 4 times, [ssk] 2 times, pm, k2—2 garter sts at center front edge, 1 marked full 25-st rep of feather and fan patt, (19, 22) sts in partial patt, 2 edge sts at side seam edge.

All sizes:

Row 4: Knit.

Rep Rows 1–4, working 2 sts at center front in garter st, until Rows 1–4 have been worked 14 times total—56 patt rows total; piece measures about 12" (30.5 cm) from CO for all sizes, measured straight up along the center st of main patt.

Shape Collar

Next row: (RS, Row 1 of patt) K2, yo, slip marker (sl m), work Row 1 of patt as established to end—3 sts in marked center front garter st section. Work 3 rows even in patt, ending with Row 4 and working new st in garter st. *Next row:* (RS, Row 1 of patt) K2, yo, knit to m, sl m, work Row 1 of patt as established to end—1 st inc'd in center front garter section. Cont in patt, rep the shaping of the last 4 rows 1 more time—38 (41, 44, 51, 54) sts total; 5 sts in garter st at center front. Cont in patt until 19 reps have been completed from CO, then work Rows 1–3 once more to end with a RS row—79 patt rows completed; piece measures about 17" (43 cm) from CO for all sizes measured straight up along center st of main patt.

Shape Armhole

Note: As for back armhole, discontinue the partial patt rep at side; instead, work the partial rep sts and side seam edge sts as St st on patt Rows 1–3, and knit them on patt Row 4 to form a garter ridge to match the feather and fan patt. BO 4 (4, 5, 5, 7) sts at beg of next WS row (Row 4 of patt)—34 (37, 39, 46, 47) sts rem; 4 (7, 9, 16, 17) sts on side seam edge of main

patt. Work Row 1 of patt even. Cont as established, dec 1 st each end of needle on next 3 RS rows, ending with Row 3 of patt—31 (34, 36, 43, 44) sts rem; 1 (4, 6, 13, 14) st(s) on side seam edge of patt. Work 3 rows even, ending with Row 2 of patt. Reestablish patt on next row (Row 3 of patt) as foll for your size:

Sizes 33 (36, 39)" only: K5 (center front sts), work next 25 sts for feather and fan patt as [yo, k1] 4 times, [ssk] 4 times, k1, [k2tog] 4 times, [yo, k1] 4 times, [yo, k1] 0 (1, 2) time(s), [ssk] 0 (1, 2) time(s), k1 (1, 0)—5 garter sts at center front edge, 1 marked full 25-st rep of feather and fan patt, 0 (3, 6) sts in partial patt rep, 1 (1, 0) edge st at side seam edge.

Sizes (45½, 48½)" only: K5 (center front sts), work next 25 sts for feather and fan patt as [yo, k1] 4 times, [ssk] 4 times, k1, [k2tog] 4 times, [yo, k1] 4 times, work next (13, 14) sts as [yo, k1] (2, 3) times, [ssk] (2, 3) times, k1, [k2tog] (2, 0) times, [yo, k1] (2, 0) times, k(0, 4)—5 garter sts at center front edge, 1 marked full 25-st rep of feather and fan patt, (13, 14) sts in partial patt.

All sizes: Cont as established until armhole measures about 8 (8½, 9, 9, 9½)" (20.5 [21.5, 23, 23, 24] cm), ending with Row 2 of patt.

Shape Shoulder

Cut yarn. Work short-rows as foll:

Short-row 1: (RS) Place first 18 (18, 18, 19, 19) sts on holder for collar, rejoin yarn with RS facing, knit to last 7 (8, 9, 12, 13) sts, wrap next st, turn—13 (16, 18, 24, 25) sts rem.

Short-row 2: (WS) K6 (8, 9, 12, 12), turn.

Short-row 3: K13 (16, 18, 24, 25), working the wrapped st tog with its wrap.

Place sts on separate holder for right front shoulder.

LEFT FRONT

With smaller needles, CO 35 (38, 41, 48, 51) sts. Knit 4 rows. Change to larger needles.

Row 1: (RS) Knit.

Row 2: K2 for center front sts (work in garter st), purl to end.

Row 3: Establish patt for your size as foll:

Sizes 33 (36, 39)" only: K2 (edge sts at side seam), [k2tog] 2 (3, 4) times, [yo, k1] 2 (3, 4) times, pm, work next 25 sts for feather and fan patt as [yo, k1] 4 times, [ssk] 4 times, k1, [k2tog] 4 times, [yo, k1] 4 times, pm, k2 (center front sts)—2 edge sts at side seam, 6 (9, 12) sts for partial patt rep, 1 marked full 25-st rep of feather and fan patt, 2 garter sts at center front.

Sizes (45½, 48½)" only: K2 (side seam sts), pm, work next (19, 22) sts in modified patt as [k2tog] 2 times, [yo, k1] 4 times, [ssk] 2 times, k1, [k2tog] (2, 3) times, [yo, k1] (2, 3) times, pm, work next 25 sts for feather and fan patt as [yo, k1] 4 times, [ssk] 4 times, k1, [k2tog] 4 times, [yo, k1] 4 times, pm, k2 (center front sts)—2 edge sts at side seam; (19, 22) sts in partial patt, 1 marked full 25-st rep of feather and fan patt, 2 garter sts at center front.

All sizes:

Row 4: Knit.

Rep Rows 1–4, keeping 2 sts at center front in garter st, until Rows 1–4 have been worked 14 times total—56 patt rows total; piece measures about 12" (30.5 cm) from CO for all sizes, measured straight up along the center st of main patt.

Shape Collar

Next row: (RS, Row 1 of patt) Work in patt to last 2 sts, sl m, yo, k2—3 sts in marked center front garter st section. Work 3 rows even in patt, ending with Row 4 and working new st in garter st. *Next row:* (RS, Row 1 of patt) Work in patt to marked section for center front sts, sl m, knit to last 2 sts, yo, k2—1 st inc'd in center front garter section. Cont in patt, rep the shaping of the last 4 rows 1 more time—38 (41, 44, 51, 54) sts total; 5 sts in garter st at center front. Cont in patt until Rows 1–4 have been worked a total of 20 times, ending with Row 4—80 patt rows total; piece measures 17" (43 cm) from CO for all sizes, measured straight up along a single column of sts at center back.

Shape Armhole

Note: As for back and right front armholes, discontinue the partial patt rep at side; instead, work the partial rep sts and side seam edge sts as St st on patt Rows 1–3, and knit them on patt Row 4 to form a garter ridge to match the feather and fan patt. BO 4 (4, 5, 5, 7) sts at beg of next RS row (Row 1 of patt)—34 (37, 39, 46, 47) sts rem; 4 (7, 9, 16, 17) sts on side seam edge of main patt. Work Row 2 of patt even. Cont as established, dec 1 st each end of needle on next 3 RS rows, ending with Row 3 of patt—31 (34, 36, 43, 44) sts rem, 1 (4, 6, 13, 14) st(s) on side seam edge of patt. Work 3 rows even, ending with Row 2 of patt. Reestablish patt on next row (Row 3 of patt) as foll for your size:

Sizes 33 (36, 39)" only: K1 (1, 0), k2tog 0 (1, 2) time(s), [yo, k1] 0 (1, 2) time(s), work next 25 sts for feather and fan patt as [yo, k1] 4 times, [ssk] 4 times, k1, [k2tog] 4 times, [yo, k1] 4 times, k5 (center front sts)—1 (1, 0) edge st at side seam edge, 0 (3, 6) sts in partial patt rep, 1 marked full 25-st rep of feather and fan patt, 5 garter sts at center front edge.

Sizes (45½, 48½)" only: Work (13, 14) sts for partial patt as k(0, 4), [k1, yo] (2, 0) times, [ssk] (2, 0) times, k1, [k2tog] (2, 3) times, [yo, k1] (2, 3) times, work next 25 sts for feather and fan patt as [yo, k1] 4 times, [ssk] 4 times, k1, [k2tog] 4 times, [yo, k1] 4 times; k5 (center front

sts)—(13, 14) sts in partial patt, 1 marked full 25-st rep of feather and fan patt, 5 garter sts at center front edge. *Note:* For size 45½" the sts in the first square bracket are deliberately worked in reverse order as k1, yo instead of yo, k1 to avoid having a yo at the selvedge. **All sizes:** Cont as established until armhole measures about 8 (8½, 9, 9, 9½)" (20.5 [21.5, 23, 23, 24] cm), ending with Row 1 of patt.

Shape Shoulder

Work short-rows as foll:

Short-row 1: (WS, Row 2 of patt) K5 center front sts, p13 (13, 13, 14, 14), place 18 (18, 18, 19, 19) sts just worked on holder for collar, purl to last 7 (8, 9, 12, 13) sts, wrap next st, turn—13 (16, 18, 24, 25) sts.

Short-row 2: (RS) K6 (8, 9, 12, 12), turn.

Short-row 3: P13 (16, 18, 24, 25) to end, working the wrapped st tog with its wrap.

Place sts on holder for left front shoulder.

SLEEVES

With smaller needles, CO 36 (38, 40, 42, 44) sts. Knit 4 rows. Change to larger needles.

Row 1: (RS) Knit.

Row 2: Purl.

Row 3: K6 (7, 8, 9, 10), pm, [k2tog] 4 times, [yo, k1] 8 times, [ssk] 4 times, pm, k6 (7, 8, 9, 10).

Row 4: Knit.

Cont in patt until Rows 1–4 have been worked a total of 12 times, ending with Row 4—48 patt rows total; piece measures 10¼" (26 cm) from CO for all sizes measured straight up at center. *Inc row:* (RS, Row 1 of patt) K2, M1 (see Glossary, page 155), work in patt to last 2 sts, M1, k2—2 sts inc'd. Work new sts in St st on patt Rows 1–3, and knit them on patt Row 4 to form a garter ridge to match the feather and fan patt. Cont in patt, inc 1 st each end of needle in this manner every 8 (6, 6, 0, 0)th row 2 (5, 2, 0, 0) times, then every 6 (4, 4, 4, 4)th row 3 (1, 6, 9, 10) time(s)—48 (52, 58, 62, 66) sts. Cont as established until piece measures 19 (19, 19½, 19½, 20)" (48.5 [48.5, 49.5, 49.5, 51] cm) from CO measured straight up at center, ending with a WS row.

Shape Cap

BO 4 (4, 5, 5, 7) sts at beg of next 2 rows—40 (44, 48, 52, 52) sts rem. Dec 1 st each end of needle every other row 3 (4, 6, 14, 7) times, then every 4th row 3 (3, 2, 0, 1) time(s), then every other row 2 (3, 4, 0, 6) times—24 center patt sts rem; cap measures about 5 (5¾, 6, 6, 6½)" (12.5 [14.5, 15, 15, 16.5] cm) measured straight up at center. BO all sts.

Alternate groups of yarnovers with groups of decreases on the same row to create a scallop pattern.

FINISHING

Stretch pieces firmly to finished measurements and pin them in place. To create the effect of faux waist shaping, stretch the hem and bustline areas of back and fronts wider than waist sections. Steam-block and allow to air-dry. Place sts for right front and right back shoulders on smaller needles. Hold shoulder sts with RS facing tog and use larger needle and the three-needle method (see Glossary, page 151) to join shoulder sts tog. Join left back and left front shoulders in the same manner.

Left Collar

Return held 18 (18, 18, 19, 19) sts of left front to larger needles, and join yarn with RS facing. Reestablish patt on next row (Row 3 of patt) as foll: K1 (1, 1, 2, 2), [k2tog] 4 times, [yo, k1] 4 times, k5 (center front sts). Cont in established patt until collar extension reaches to center back neck, about 3¼ (3¼, 3¼, 3½, 3½)" (8.5 [8.5, 8.5, 9, 9] cm), ending with RS Row 3 of patt. Shape collar using short-rows as foll:

Row 1: (WS) Knit to last 6 (6, 6, 7, 7) sts, wrap next st, turn.

Row 2: (RS) Knit to end.

Row 3: P6, wrap next st, turn.

Row 4: Knit to end.

Knit across all sts, working wrapped sts tog with their wraps. Place sts on holder.

Right Collar

Return held 18 (18, 18, 19, 19) sts of right front to larger needles, and join yarn with RS facing. Reestablish patt on next row (RS; Row 3 of patt) as foll: K5 (center front sts), [yo, k1] 4 times, [ssk] 4 times, k1 (1, 1, 2, 2). Cont in established patt until collar extension reaches to center back neck, about 3¼ (3¼, 3¼, 3½, 3½)" (8.5 [8.5, 8.5, 9, 9] cm), ending with WS Row 2 of patt. Shape collar using short-rows as foll:

Row 1: (RS) Knit to last 6 (6, 6, 7, 7) sts, wrap next st, turn.

Row 2: (WS) Knit to end.

Row 3: K6, wrap next st, turn.

Row 4: Purl to end.

Knit across all sts, working wrapped sts tog with their wraps. Return held sts of left collar to smaller needle. Hold ends of collar tog with WS facing tog and use larger needle and the three-needle method to join ends of collar tog; the welt from the join will be on the RS of the body but will not show on the public side of the garment when the collar is folded back. With yarn threaded on a tapestry needle, sew collar selvedge to back neck. Sew sleeves into armholes. Sew sleeve and side seams. Weave in loose ends. Lightly block seams again.

OOH LA LACE DRESS AND STOLE

SHIRLEY PADEN

In this elegant dress and stole ensemble, **Shirley Paden** proves that sometimes you can't have too much of a good thing. She chose a relatively large lace pattern as the allover design for a body-hugging and curve-revealing dress and repeated it on the accompanying stole. To simplify the knitting and to avoid introducing an element that might interfere with the lace pattern in the body of the dress, Shirley used different needle sizes (and therefore different gauges) to shape the hips, waist, and bust. The dress closes at the back with ten tiny buttons; a slit at the back hem facilitates walking while maintaining the slim fit.

NEEDLES

Dress—4 or 5 pairs of straight needles (depending on your size) as foll:

Small: Sizes 9 (5.5 mm), 8 (5 mm), 7 (4.5 mm), 6 (4 mm), and 4 (3.5 mm).

Medium: Sizes 9 (5.5 mm), 8 (5 mm), 7 (4.5 mm), and 5 (3.75 mm).

Large: Sizes 8 (5 mm), 7 (4.5 mm), 6 (4 mm), 5 (3.75 mm), and 4 (3.5 mm).

Extra Large: Sizes 8 (5 mm), 7 (4.5 mm), 6 (4 mm), and 5 (3.75 mm).

Stole—Size 8 (5 mm): straight. Adjust needle size if necessary to obtain the correct gauge.

NOTIONS

A few yards (meters) of smooth contrasting waste yarn for measuring gauge and for holding stole sts; markers (m); tapestry needle; stitch holders; size D/3 (3.25 mm) crochet hook; thirteen ½" (1.3 cm) buttons (10 for back opening, 3 for lower back slit).

GAUGE

See Notes for instructions on how to work the gauge swatch. In Closed Bud pattern from chart, after blocking:

45 stitches = 10½" (26.5 cm) and 52 rows = 7" (18 cm) on size 9 (5.5 mm) needles.

45 stitches = 9½" (24 cm) and 52 rows = 7" (18 cm) on size 8 (5 mm) needles.

45 stitches = 8½" (21.5 cm) and 52 rows = 6¾" (17 cm) on size 7 (4.5 mm) needles.

45 stitches = 8" (20.5 cm) and 52 rows = 6¾" (17 cm) on size 6 (4 mm) needles.

45 stitches = 7¾" (19.5 cm) and 52 rows = 6½" (16.5 cm) on size 5 (3.75 mm) needles.

45 stitches = 7½" (19 cm) and 52 rows = 6½" (16.5 cm) on size 4 (3.5 mm) needles.

FINISHED SIZE

Dress: Small (Medium, Large, Extra Large), 37½ (41, 42, 47)" (95 [104, 106.5, 119.5] cm) bust and hip circumference; 29½ (30½, 37, 38½)" (75 [77.5, 94, 98] cm) waist circumference; and 48¼ (48½, 46¾, 48¼)" (122.5 [123, 118.5, 122.5] cm) from lower edge to shoulders with dress measured flat; dress will hang about 3½" (9 cm) longer when worn (see Notes). Shown in size 37½" (95 cm) bust and hip.

Stole: 23½" (59.5 cm) wide and 70" (178 cm) long, not including knotted fringe. Fringe will add 7" (18 cm) at each end; stole will stretch slightly in length when worn.

YARN

DK weight (CYCA #3 Light).

Shown here: Blue Sky Alpacas Alpaca Silk (50% alpaca, 50% silk; 146 yd [133 m]/ 50 g): #137 sapphire (aqua); 13 (14, 15, 16) skeins for dress, 11 skeins for stole.

NOTES

❖ Beginning with the largest needles for your size, work a gauge swatch on 47 stitches as follows: 1 selvedge stitch (knit every row), work 45 stitches in pattern from Closed Bud chart, 1 selvedge stitch (knit every row). Work two complete pattern repeats (52 rows), then use a smooth, contrasting waste yarn to baste across the last row. Change to the next size smaller needles, work another two complete pattern repeats, then baste across the last row again. Continue in this manner, changing to the next smaller needles after every two pattern repeats, until you have used all the needles for your size. Bind off all stitches. Block the finished swatch strip, then measure the gauge for each needle size from the marked sections of the blocked swatch, measuring inside the selvedge stitches; do not include the selvedge stitches in determining the gauge.

❖ The waist, hip, and bust shaping are achieved by changing needle sizes. Pay close attention to where the needle sizes change, and make sure to change both needles.

❖ Measure the length of the work in progress with the knitting lying flat. When worn, the dress will hang to about 3½" (9 cm) longer than the flat length.

❖ The instructions for the dress body contain an exact number of rows for a total planned length of 48¼ (48½, 46¾, 48¼)" (122.5 [123, 118.5, 122.5] cm) from cast on to shoulder, measured with the knitting lying flat. To lengthen or shorten the dress, add or remove complete 26-row pattern repeats just below the hip-to-waist shaping, and above where the two halves of the lower back join for the back slit in order to maintain the full length of the slit. Every 26 rows added or removed will lengthen or shorten the dress by about 3½ (3½, 3⅜, 3½)" (9 [9, 8.5, 9] cm).

❖ Knit the first and last stitch of every row for selvedge stitches; these selvedge stitches are not shown on the chart and are not included in calculating the measurements shown on the schematic.

❖ When shaping, maintain the established pattern as much as possible. If there are not enough stitches available as a result of shaping to work every yarnover with its companion decrease(s), work the stitches in stockinette instead until the stitch count can accommodate working in pattern again.

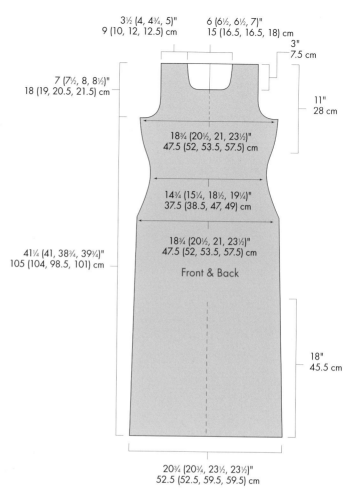

3½ (4, 4¾, 5)"
9 (10, 12, 12.5) cm

6 (6½, 6½, 7)"
15 (16.5, 16.5, 18) cm

3"
7.5 cm

7 (7½, 8, 8½)"
18 (19, 20.5, 21.5) cm

11"
28 cm

18¾ (20½, 21, 23½)"
47.5 (52, 53.5, 57.5) cm

14¾ (15¼, 18½, 19¼)"
37.5 (38.5, 47, 49) cm

41¼ (41, 38¾, 39¼)"
105 (104, 98.5, 101) cm

18¾ (20½, 21, 23½)"
47.5 (52, 53.5, 57.5) cm

Front & Back

18"
45.5 cm

20¾ (20¾, 23½, 23½)"
52.5 (52.5, 59.5, 59.5) cm

Closed Bud

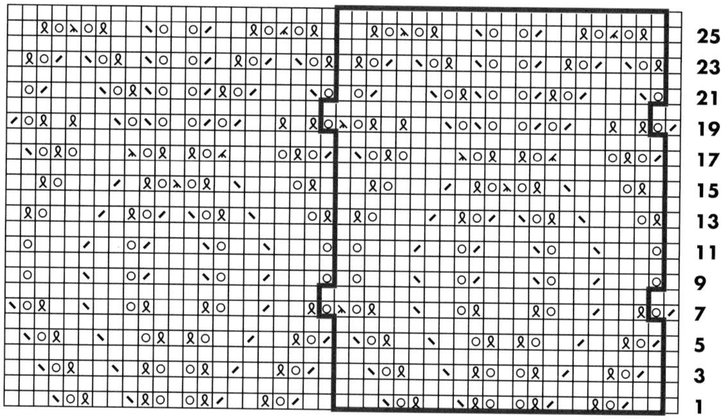

selvedge sts not shown

Symbol	Meaning	Symbol	Meaning	Symbol	Meaning
□	k on RS; p on WS	╱	k2tog	⋏	sl 1, k2tog, psso
ℓ	k1 tbl	╲	ssk	☐	pattern repeat
○	yo	⋌	k3tog		

STITCH GUIDE

K2, P2 Rib: (multiple of 4 sts + 2)

Row 1: K1 (selvedge st; knit every row), p1, *k2, p2; rep from * to last 4 sts, k2, p1, k1 (selvedge st; knit every row).

Row 2: K1 (selvedge st), k1, *p2, k2; rep from * to last 4 sts, p2, k1, k1 (selvedge st).

Repeat Rows 1 and 2 for pattern.

Sloped Bind-Off: On the row before binding off, do not work the last st of the row. Turn work—1 unworked st on right needle. To bind off, sl first st on left needle to right needle as if to purl, then pass the unworked st over it to BO 1 st. BO the next sts in the usual manner. *Note:* This technique is used only for the first st of each group of BO sts to prevent "stair steps" along the shaped edge when working multiple sets of bind-offs.

DRESS FRONT

With size 9 (9, 8, 8) (5.5 [5.5, 5, 5] mm) needles, CO 91 (91, 113, 113) sts. *Next row:* (WS) K1 (selvedge st), purl to last st, k1 (selvedge st). *Next row:* (RS) Establish patt from Closed Bud chart as foll: K1 (selvedge st), work Row 1 of Closed Bud chart over center 89 (89, 111, 111) sts, k1 (selvedge st). Working 1 selvedge st at each end of needle, work Rows 2–26 of chart once—piece measures 3½" (9 cm) from CO for all sizes.

Sizes small (large) only: Change to size 8 (7) (5 [4.5] mm) needles.

All sizes: Rep Rows 1–26 of chart 7 (7, 6, 6) more times, then work Rows 1–4 (1–2, 1–18, 1–18) once more—212 (210, 200, 200) patt rows total from CO; piece measures 28½ (28¼, 26, 27)" (72.5 [72, 66, 68.5] cm) from CO.

Shape Hip to Waist

Keeping in patt, change to size 7 (8, 6, 7) (4.5 [5, 4, 4.5] mm) needles and work 20 rows, ending with Row 24 (22, 12, 12) of chart. Change to size 6 (7, 5, 6) (4 [4.5, 3.75, 4] mm) needles and work 20 (20, 22, 20) more rows, ending with Row 18 (16, 8, 6) of chart—piece measures 33¾ (33½, 31¼, 32¼)" (85.5 [85, 79.5, 82] cm) from CO.

Waist

Keeping in patt, change to size 4 (5, 4, 5) (3.5 [3.75, 3.5, 3.75] mm) needles and work even for 12 rows, ending with Row 4 (2, 20, 18) of chart—piece measures 35¼ (35, 32¾, 33¾)" (89.5 [89, 83, 85.5] cm) from CO.

Worked in rounds, a lace pattern has no beginning and no end.

Shape Waist to Bust

Keeping in patt, change to size 6 (7, 5, 6) (4 [4.5, 3.75, 4] mm) needles and work 16 rows, ending with Row 20 (18, 10, 8) of chart. Change to size 7 (8, 6, 7) (4.5 [5, 4, 4.5] mm) needles and work 16 more rows, ending with Row 10 (8, 26, 24) of chart. Change to size 8 (9, 7, 8) (5 [5.5, 4.5, 5] mm) needles and work 14 (14, 16, 14) more rows, ending with Row 24 (22, 16, 12) of chart—310 (308, 302, 298) patt rows total; eleven 26-row reps plus 24 (22, 16, 12) rows; piece measures 41¼ (41, 38¾, 39¾)" (105 [104, 98.5, 101] cm) from CO.

Shape Armholes

Change to size 7 (8, 6, 7) (4.5 [5, 4, 4.5] mm) needles. Keeping in patt, BO 3 sts at beg of next 2 rows, then BO 2 sts at beg of foll 6 rows, then BO 1 st at beg of foll 4 rows—69 (69, 91, 91) sts rem; 322 (320, 314, 310) patt rows total. Cont even in patt for 18 (20, 26, 30) more rows, ending with Row 2 of chart—340 rows total for all sizes; piece measures 45¼ (45½, 43¾, 45¼)" (115 [115.5, 111, 115] cm) from CO.

Shape Neck

Next row: (RS) Work 26 (26, 36, 36) sts in patt, join a second ball of yarn and BO center 17 (17, 19, 19) sts, work in patt to end—26 (26, 36, 36) sts rem at each side. Keeping in patt and working each side separately, use the sloped bind-off technique (see Stitch Guide) to BO 1 (1, 2, 2) st(s) at each neck edge on next row, then BO 1 st at each neck edge every other row 6 (6, 7, 7) more times—19 (19, 27, 27) sts rem each side. Work even until Row 26 of 14th patt rep has been completed—364 rows for all sizes; armholes measure 7 (7½, 8, 8½)" (18 [19, 20.5, 21.5] cm); piece measures 48¼ (48½, 46¾, 48¼)" (122.5 [123, 118.5, 122.5] cm) from CO. Place sts on holders.

DRESS BACK

Lower Left Side

With size 9 (9, 8, 8) (5.5 [5.5, 5, 5] mm) needles, CO 47 (47, 58, 58) sts. *Next row:* (WS) K1 (selvedge st), purl to last st, k1 (selvedge st). *Next row:* (RS) Establish patt from Row 1 of Closed Bud chart as foll for your size:

Sizes small and medium: K1 (selvedge st), work patt from chart over center 45 sts, k1 (selvedge st).

Sizes large and extra large: K1 (selvedge st), work from the 11th st of the patt rep box to end of patt rep box once (12 sts), work 22-st patt once, work 22 sts after patt rep box once, k1 (selvedge st). Do not work any decreases or yarnovers without their companions in order to maintain consistent st count (see Notes).

Wear a contrasting colored bodysuit under this dress for a more playful look.

All sizes: Working in patt as established for your size, work Rows 2–26 of chart once—piece measures 3½" (9 cm) from CO for all sizes.

Sizes small (large) only: Change to size 8 (7) (5 [4.5] mm) needles.

All sizes: Rep Rows 1–26 of chart 4 more times, then work Rows 1–2 (2, 6, 2) once—132 (132, 136, 132) patt rows total from CO. *Next row:* (RS) K1 (selvedge st), k2tog, work in patt to end—46 (46, 57, 57) sts. *Next row:* (WS) Work in patt to last 3 sts, p2tog, k1 (selvedge st)—45 (45, 56, 56) sts; 134 (134, 138, 134) patt rows total; piece measures 18" (45.5 cm) from CO for all sizes. Place sts on holder.

Lower Right Side

With size 9 (9, 8, 8) (5.5 [5.5, 5, 5] mm) needles, CO 47 (47, 58, 58) sts. *Next row:* (WS) K1 (selvedge st), purl to last st, k1 (selvedge st). *Next row:* (RS) Establish patt from Row 1 of Closed Bud chart as foll for your size:

Sizes small and medium: K1 (selvedge st), work patt from chart over center 45 sts, k1 (selvedge st).

Sizes large and extra large: K1 (selvedge st), work 1 st before patt rep box, rep 22-st patt 2 times, work 11 sts after patt rep box once, k1 (selvedge st). Do not work any decreases or yarnovers without their companions in order to maintain consistent st count.

All sizes: Working in patt as established for your size, work Rows 2–26 of chart once—piece measures 3½" (9 cm) from CO for all sizes.

Sizes small (large) only: Change to size 8 (7) (5 [4.5] mm) needles.

All sizes: Rep Rows 1–26 of chart 4 more times, then work Row 1–2 (2, 6, 2) once—132 (132, 136, 132) patt rows total from CO. *Next row:* (RS) Work in patt to last 3 sts, ssk, k1 (selvedge st)—46 (46, 57, 57) sts. *Next row:* (WS) Work even in patt—134 (134, 138, 134) patt rows total; piece measures 18" (45.5 cm) from CO for all sizes. Leave sts on needle.

Join Right and Left Sides

Next row: (RS; Row 5 [5, 9, 5] of chart) Work in patt across 46 (46, 57, 57) sts of lower right side, return 45 (45, 56, 56) held sts of lower left side to needles with RS facing, work in patt to end—91 (91, 113, 113) sts. Work 77 (75, 61, 65) more rows in patt, ending with Row 4 (2, 18, 18) of chart—212 (210, 200, 200) patt rows total from CO; piece measures 28½ (28¼, 26, 27)" (72.5 [72, 66, 68.5] cm) from CO.

Shape Hip to Waist

Keeping in patt, change to size 7 (8, 6, 7) (4.5 [5, 4, 4.5] mm) needles and work 20 rows, ending with Row 24 (22, 12, 12) of chart. Change to size 6 (7, 5, 6) (4 [4.5, 3.75, 4] mm)

Think about scale— large motifs look best in large areas; small motifs look best in small ones.

needles and work 20 (20, 22, 20) more rows, ending with Row 18 (16, 8, 6) of chart—piece measures 33¾ (33½, 31¼, 32¼)" (85.5 [85, 79.5, 82] cm) from CO.

Waist

Keeping in patt, change to size 4 (5, 4, 5) (3.5 [3.75, 3.5, 3.75] mm) needles and work even for 12 rows, ending with Row 4 (2, 20, 18) of chart—piece measures 35¼ (35, 32¾, 33¾)" (89.5 [89, 83, 85.5] cm) from CO.

Shape Waist to Bust

Note: The back opening measures 11" (28 cm) long from the shoulder line for all sizes and begins 4 (3½, 3, 2½)" (10 [9, 7.5, 6.5] cm) below start of armhole shaping. Divide for the back opening while cont the waist to bust shaping for your size as foll:

Size small: Keeping in patt, change to size 6 (4 mm) needles and work 15 rows, ending with RS Row 19 of chart. *Next row:* (WS; Row 20 of chart) K1, p44, p1f&b (see Glossary, page 156) in center st placing a marker between the 2 sts created from the center st to mark the exact center of the back, p44, k1—92 sts. Change to size 7 (4.5 mm) needles. *Next row:* (RS; Row 21 of chart) Work 45 sts in patt, k1f&b (see Glossary, page 155), join a second ball of yarn, k1f&b, work 45 sts in patt—47 sts at each side. Working each side separately and knitting the first and last st of each side for selvedge sts, work 15 more rows, ending with Row 10 of chart. Change to size 8 (5 mm) needles and work 14 more rows, ending with Row 24 of chart.

Size medium: Keeping in patt, change to size 7 (4.5 mm) needles and work 16 rows, ending with Row 18 of chart. Change to size 8 (5 mm) needles and work 3 rows, ending with RS Row 21 of chart. *Next row:* (WS; Row 22 of chart) K1, p44, p1f&b (see Glossary, page 156) in center st placing a marker between the 2 sts created from the center st to mark the exact center of the back, p44, k1—92 sts. *Next row:* (RS; Row 23 of chart) Work 45 sts in patt, k1f&b (see Glossary, page 155), join a second ball of yarn, k1f&b, work 45 sts in patt—47 sts at each side. Working each side separately and knitting the first and last st of each side for selvedge sts, work 11 more rows, ending with Row 8 of chart. Change to size 9 (5.5 mm) needles and work 14 more rows, ending with Row 22 of chart.

Size large: Keeping in patt, change to size 5 (3.75 mm) needles and work 16 rows, ending with Row 10 of chart. Change to size 6 (4 mm) needles and work 7 rows, ending with RS Row 17 of chart. *Next row:* (WS; Row 18 of chart) K1, p55, p1f&b (see Glossary, page 156) in center st placing a marker between the 2 sts created from the center st to mark the exact center of the back, p55, k1—114 sts. *Next row:* (RS; Row 19 of chart) Work 56 sts in patt, k1f&b (see Glossary, page 155), join a second ball of yarn, k1f&b, work 56 sts in patt—58 sts at each side. Working each side separately and knitting the first and last sts of each side for selvedge sts, work 7 more rows, ending with Row 26 of chart. Change to size 7 (4.5 mm) needles and work 16 more rows, ending with Row 16 of chart.

Size extra large: Keeping in patt, change to size 6 (4 mm) needles and work 16 rows, ending with Row 8 of chart. Change to size 7 (4.5 mm) needles and work 9 rows, ending with RS Row 17 of chart. *Next row:* (WS; Row 18 of chart) K1, p55, p1f&b (see Glossary, page 156) in center st placing a marker between the 2 sts created from the center st to mark the exact center of the back, p55, k1—114 sts. *Next row:* (RS; Row 19 of chart) Work 56 sts in patt, k1f&b (see Glossary, page 155), join a second ball of yarn, k1f&b, work 56 sts in patt—58 sts at each side. Working each side separately and knitting the first and last st of each side for selvedge sts, work 5 more rows, ending with Row 24 of chart. Change to size 8 (5 mm) needles and work 14 more rows, ending with Row 12 of chart.

All sizes: After completing waist to bust shaping—47 (47, 58, 58) sts at each side; 310 (308, 302, 298) patt rows total; eleven 26-row reps plus 24 (22, 16, 12) rows; piece measures 41¼ (41, 38¾, 39¾)" (105 [104, 98.5, 101] cm) from CO.

Shape Armholes

Change to size 7 (8, 6, 7) (4.5 [5, 4, 4.5] mm) needles. Keeping in patt and working each side separately, at each armhole edge BO 3 sts once, then BO 2 sts 3 times, then BO 1 st 2 times—36 (36, 47, 47) sts rem each side. Cont even in patt until Row 26 of 14th patt rep has been completed—364 rows for all sizes; armholes measure 7 (7½, 8, 8½)" (18 [19, 20.5, 21.5] cm); piece measures 48¼ (48½, 46¾, 48¼)" (122.5 [123, 118.5, 122.5] cm) from CO. Place sts on holders.

FINISHING

Block pieces to measurements. Place sts for right front and right back shoulders on separate size 6 (7, 5, 6) (4 [4.5, 3.75, 4] mm) needles. Holding shoulder sts with RS touching and WS facing out, use a size 7 (8, 6, 7) (4.5 [5, 4, 4.5] cm) needle and the three-needle method (see Glossary, page 151) to BO shoulder sts tog, then with same needle BO rem back neck sts. Join back and front at left shoulder in the same manner.

Neckband

With size 5 (3.75 mm) needles, RS facing, and beg at neck edge of left back, pick up and knit 114 (114, 118, 118) sts evenly spaced around neck opening. Work k2, p2 rib (see Stitch Guide) until piece measures 5" (12.5 cm) from pick-up row, ending with a WS row. *Next row:* (RS) Keeping in patt, work 28 (28, 29, 29) sts, BO center 58 (58, 60, 60) sts, work to end—28 (28, 29, 29) sts at each side. Working sts for the right side of the neck where the yarn is attached, at neck edge (beg of RS rows), BO 14 (14, 15, 15) sts once, then BO 14 sts once. Rejoin yarn to sts for left side of neck with WS facing. At neck edge (beg of WS rows), BO 14 (14, 15, 15) sts once, then BO 14 sts once.

Neck Edging

With crochet hook, RS facing, and beg at top of right back neckband, work 1 row of single crochet (sc; see Glossary, page 154, for crochet instructions) around back opening as foll: 66 sc from top of neckband to base of opening, 3 sc across bottom of opening, 66 sc from to top of left back neckband—135 sc total. Cut yarn. Rejoin yarn to top of right back neckband with WS facing, and work 1 row of reverse single crochet (rev sc) around opening as foll to create 10 button loops along the right side of opening: Work 1 rev sc in first sc, *work 1 sl st in next sc, ch 9, work 1 sl st in same sc as before, work 1 rev sc in each of next 6 sc; rep from * 8 more times, work 1 sl st in next sc, ch 9, work 1 sl st in same sc as before, ch-9 to make 1 button loop (10 button loops completed), work 1 rev sc next sc, work 1 rev sc in each sc across bottom of opening, then work 1 rev sc in each of sc to top of left back neckband. Fasten off last st.

Slit Edging

With crochet hook, RS facing, and beg at bottom of left back, work 2 rows of sc as foll: 75 sts from lower edge to ½" (1.3 mm) below top of slit, 4 sc to center top, 1 sc in center, 4 sc along top ½" (1.3 mm) of right back, 75 sts to bottom of right back—159 sc. *Next row:* (RS) Work 1 sl st in first sc, *ch 3, skip 1 sc, work 1 sl st in each of next 3 sc*; rep from * to * 19 times total, work 1 sl st in each of rem 2 sc at top of slit, work 1 sl st in center top sc, work 1 sl st in each of the first 5 sc along right side of slit, rep from * to * 18 times total, end ch 3, skip 1 sc, work 1 sl st in rem sc. Fasten off last st.

Armhole Edging

With crochet hook, RS facing, and beg at base of armhole, work 67 (71, 75, 79) sc evenly spaced around armhole. Join for working in the rnd, and work 1 more rnd of sc. *Next rnd:* *Work 1 sl st in each of next 3 sc, ch 3, skip 1 sc*; rep from * 16 (17, 18, 19) times total, work 1 sl st in each of rem 3 sc. Fasten off last st. Rep for other armhole.

Buttons

Sew 10 buttons to left side of back opening, opposite button loops. Sew 3 buttons to top of left side of slit, opposite the first, third, and fifth picots of the right side. Use the picot chains of the slit edging as button loops to button the slit closed as desired.

STOLE

Note: Stole is made in two identical halves, each knitted from the outer edge to the center, which are grafted together at the center during finishing.

A row (or two) of crochet makes an inconspicuous edging.

First Half

With size 8 (5 mm) needles, CO 113 sts. *Next row:* (WS) K1 (selvedge st), purl to last st, k1 (selvedge st). *Next row:* (RS) Establish patt from Closed Bud chart as foll: K1 (selvedge st), work Row 1 of Closed Bud chart over center 111 sts, k1 (selvedge st). Knitting the first and last st of every row for selvedges, work in patt until 10 reps total of 26-row chart have been completed—260 patt rows; piece measures 35" (89 cm) from CO. Place sts on waste yarn.

Second Half

Work as for first half, ending with Row 25 of the 10th patt rep—259 patt rows. The grafted join in the center of the stole will substitute for the final WS row of this side. Place sts on waste yarn.

Finishing

Block pieces to measurements. Place sts for each half on separate needles and hold pieces with WS touching, RS facing outwards, and the needle with only 259 patt rows in front. Thread a tapestry needle with a length of yarn 3 to 4 times the width of the stole. Using the Kitchener stitch (see Glossary, page 155), graft the sts tog all the way across, adjusting the tension of the grafting sts to match the knitting so the join is smooth and invisible on both RS and WS. Weave in loose ends.

Edging: With crochet hook, work 1 row sc, then 1 row rev sc (see Glossary, page 154, for crochet instructions) along each long edge of stole. Work 1 row of 124 sc (about 12 sc for every 11 sts CO) across each short edge of stole.

Fringe: Cut 204 strands of yarn 24" (61 cm) in length. Beg at one corner, apply fringes to short edge of stole as foll: Fold one group of 6 strands in half, use crochet hook to pull loop through sc in corner, pull the 12 yarn ends through loop and tighten. Attach 16 more 6-strand fringes evenly spaced along the same short end, about 7 to 8 sc apart, ending with the last fringe in last sc at other corner—17 fringe bundles on each side. Tie 2 rows of fringe knots on each short side as foll:

Row 1: Beg at one edge, divide the first pair of fringes into 2 groups of 6 strands each. Skip the first 6-strand half of the edge fringe and tie 6 strands each from the first and second fringes in an overhand knot about 1½" (3.8 cm) down from edge of stole. Rep across, tying 6 strands from each pair of fringes tog until you reach the other side; the last 6-strand half of the final edge fringe will not be knotted.

Row 2: Tie another row of overhand knots about 1½" (3.8 cm) below the previous row, this time tying the fringes in their original 12-strand groups. Trim ends even to about 7" (18 cm) long.

Change needle sizes to widen or narrow a lace pattern without working additional increases or decreases.

A wardrobe mainstay of the 1940s and 1950s, shrugs helped ensure warmth when sleek, backless dresses were all the rage. Because good ideas don't go out of fashion, shrugs remain popular accessories today. **Mercedes Tarasovich-Clark** worked this shrug from cuff to cuff in a two-row brioche stitch that's more closely related to ribbing than to traditional lace. Worked on relatively large needles throughout, the pattern takes on a lacelike appearance, especially where it stretches across the shoulders. Mercedes worked the entire body of the shrug on a consistent number of stitches but shaped the curved lower back and neck edges by changing needle sizes.

STITCH GUIDE

Brioche Lace Pattern: (even number of sts)
Row 1: (RS) K2, *yo, ssk; rep from * to last 2 sts, k2.
Row 2: (WS) P2, *yo, p2tog; rep from * to last 2 sts, p2.
Repeat Rows 1 and 2 for pattern.

SHRUG

With smallest straight needles (size 8 [5 mm] or your equivalent), CO 38 (42, 46) sts.
Row 1: (RS) *K2, p2; rep from * to last 2 sts, k2.
Row 2: (WS) *P2, k2; rep from * to last 2 sts, p2.
Rep Rows 1 and 2 until piece measures 3½" (9 cm) from CO. Change to next size larger needles (size 9 [5.5 mm]) and rep Rows 1 and 2 of brioche lace patt (see Stitch Guide) until piece measures 6 (6½, 7)" (15 [16.5, 18] cm) from CO, ending with a WS row. Change to next size larger needles (size 10 [6 mm]) and cont in patt as established until piece measures 8 (9, 10)" (20.5 [23, 25.5] cm) from CO, ending with a WS row. Mark each selvedge edge with removable marker or safety pin to indicate sleeve seam placement. Change to largest needles (size 10½ [6.5 mm]) and cont in patt until piece measures 30 (33, 36)" (76 [84, 91.5] cm)

FINISHED SIZE
About 38 (42, 46)" (96.5 [106.5, 117] cm) long from cuff to cuff, and 17½ (19, 20¼)" (44.5 [48.5, 51.5] cm) tall at center back, including ribbed edging with collar folded back. Shown in 42" (106.5 cm) length.

YARN
Worsted weight (CYCA #4 Medium).
Shown here: Classic Elite Allure (50% merino; 25% cashmere, 25% angora; 110 yd [100 m]/50 g): #10307 orange, 3 (4, 5) skeins.

NEEDLES
Sizes 8, 9, 10, and 10½ (5, 5.5, 6, and 6.5 mm): straight. Ribbing—size 8 (5 mm): 24" (60 cm) circular (cir). Adjust needle size if necessary to obtain the correct gauge.

NOTIONS
Removable markers (m) or safety pins; tapestry needle.

GAUGE
12 stitches and 16 rows = 4" (10 cm) in brioche lace pattern on largest needles, slightly stretched.

from CO, ending with a WS row. Mark each selvedge edge as before for sleeve placement. Change to next size smaller needles (size 10 [6 mm]) and cont in patt until piece measures 32 (35½, 39)" (81.5 [90, 99] cm) from CO, ending with a WS row. Change to next size smaller needles (size 9 [5.5 mm]) and cont in patt until piece measures 34½ (38½, 42½)" (87.5 [98, 108] cm) from CO. Change to small-est straight needles and work in k2, p2 rib as before for 3½" (9 cm)—piece measures 38 (42, 46)" (96.5 [106.5, 117] cm) from CO. Loosely BO all sts in patt.

FINISHING

Fold piece in half lengthwise. With yarn threaded on a tapestry needle, sew sleeve seams from ends to cuff markers—about 8 (9, 10)" (20.5 [23, 25.5] cm). Weave in loose ends.

Edging

Mark center of one long side with remov-able marker or safety pin to indicate cen-ter back neck. Place 2 more removable markers on same long side, each 4 (5, 6)" (10 [12.5, 15] cm) away from center back marker. With cir needle, RS facing, and beg at marker before center back marker, pick up and knit 16 (20, 24) sts to center marker, then 16 (20, 24) sts to next marker—32 (40, 48) sts total between outer markers. Work short-rows to shape collar while picking up additional sts around opening as foll:

Set-up row: (WS) Sl 1, p1, *k2, p2; rep from * to last 2 sts, k2, pick up and purl (see Glossary, page 156) 2 sts from long side of shrug, turn work—34 (42, 50) sts.

Row 1: Sl 1, k1, cont in rib as established to end, pick up and knit 2 sts, turn—2 sts inc'd.

Row 2: Sl 1, k1, cont in rib to end, pick up and purl 2 sts, turn—2 sts inc'd.

Row 3: Sl 1, p1, cont in rib to end, pick up and knit 2 sts, turn—2 sts inc'd.

Row 4: Sl 1, p1, cont in rib to end, pick up and purl 2 sts, turn—2 sts inc'd.

Rep Rows 1–4 three more times (do not rep set-up row)—66 (74, 82) sts. With RS facing, sl 1, work next 65 (73, 81) sts in established rib, pick up and knit 10 sts to sleeve seam, pick up and knit 94 (102, 110) sts across other long side of opening, pick up and knit 10 sts from second sleeve seam to beg of established rib sts—180 (196, 212) sts. Place marker (pm) and join for working in the rnd. Cont in rib as established until edging measures 2½" (6.5 cm) from joining rnd and about 5" (12.5 cm) tall at center back neck. Loosely BO all sts. Weave in loose ends. Block lightly to measurements.

KATHARINE HEPBURN CARDIGAN
KATHY ZIMMERMAN

Lace and cables. Cables and lace. However you pair the two, you're bound to come up with a winning combination. **Kathy Zimmerman** interpreted this classic combo in two lengths—cropped and hip—in this year-round cardigan. For both versions, Kathy followed typical 1950s styling, including a narrow fit, high round neckline, and three-quarter-length sleeves with set-in shoulders. Lots of buttons keep the fronts closed without gaps. Both versions shown here are knitted in a soft merino yarn in rich jewel tones. Choose softer shades for a more subdued look.

> **NOTES**
> ❖ When decreasing or increasing, maintain the established pattern as much as possible. If there are not enough stitches available as a result of shaping to work every yarnover with its companion decrease, work the stitches in stockinette instead until the stitch count can accommodate working in pattern again.
> ❖ Knit the first and last stitch of every row for selvedge stitches; these stitches are not shown on the charts.

BACK

With smaller needles, CO 115 (133, 147, 167, 185) sts. *Set-up row:* (WS) K1 (selvedge st; knit every row), beg as indicated for your size, work set-up row of Back chart (see page 81) over center 113 (131, 145, 165, 183) sts, k1 (selvedge st; knit every row). Knitting selvedge sts every row, work through WS Rib Row 8 of chart—piece measures about 1" (2.5 cm) from CO. Change to larger needles. *Next row:* (RS) Rep Rows 1–12 of Back chart (*do not* rep set-up or rib rows) until piece measures 6 (6, 6, 6½, 7)" (15 [15, 15, 16.5, 18] cm) from CO for short version or 13½ (13½, 14, 14½, 15)" (34.5 [34.5, 35.5, 37, 38] cm) from CO for long version ending with a WS row.

Shape Armholes

BO 6 (8, 8, 9, 10) sts at beg of next 2 rows—103 (117, 131, 149, 165) sts rem. BO 2 sts at beg of next 0 (0, 4, 6, 8) rows, then dec 1 st each end of needle every RS row 5 (7, 5, 5, 5) times—93 (103, 113, 127, 139) sts rem. Cont in patt as established until armholes measure 7 (7½, 8, 8½, 9)" (18 [19, 20.5, 21.5, 23] cm), ending with a WS row.

FINISHED SIZE
32 (36½, 40½, 46, 51)" (81.5 [92.5, 103, 117, 129.5] cm) chest/bust circumference, buttoned. Sweaters shown measure 32" (81.5 cm) in short version and 36½" (91.5 cm) in long version.

YARN
Sportweight (CYCA #2 Fine).

Shown here: Louet Sales Gems Opal (100% merino wool; 225 yd [206 m]/100 g): #62 citrus orange, 4 (5, 6, 7, 8) skeins for short version; #11 cherry red, 6 (7, 8, 9, 10) skeins for long version.

NEEDLES
Body and sleeves—size 5 (3.75 mm). Ribbing—size 4 (3.5 mm). Adjust needle size if necessary to obtain the correct gauge.

NOTIONS
Cable needle (cn); tapestry needle; seven (seven, seven, eight, eight) ⅝" (1.5 cm) buttons for short version; eleven (eleven, eleven, twelve, twelve) ⅝" (1.5 cm) buttons for long version.

GAUGE
29 stitches and 34 rows = 4" (10 cm) in cables and lace pattern from charts.

Shape Shoulders

Keeping in patt, BO 5 (7, 7, 9, 10) sts at beg of next 4 rows, then BO 6 (7, 8, 9, 11) sts at beg of foll 2 rows, then BO 6 (6, 8, 10, 11) sts at beg of foll 2 rows—49 (49, 53, 53, 55) sts rem. BO all sts.

RIGHT FRONT

With smaller needles, CO 55 (64, 71, 81, 90) sts. *Set-up row:* (WS) K1 (selvedge st; knit every row), beg and ending as indicated for your size, work set-up row of Right Front and Right Sleeve chart (see page 82) over center 53 (62, 69, 79, 88) sts, k1 (selvedge st; knit every row). Knitting selvedge sts every row, work through WS Rib Row 8 of chart. Change to larger needles. *Next row:* (RS) Rep Rows 1–12 of Right Front and Right Sleeve chart (*do not* rep set-up or rib rows) until piece measures 6 (6, 6, 6½, 7)" (15 [15, 15, 16.5, 18] cm) from CO for short version or 13½ (13½, 14, 14½, 15)" (34.5 [34.5, 35.5, 37, 38] cm) from CO for long version, ending with a RS row.

Shape Armhole

BO 6 (8, 8, 9, 10) sts at beg of next WS row—49 (56, 63, 72, 80) sts rem. BO 2 sts at beg of next 0 (0, 2, 3, 4) WS rows, then dec 1 st at end of next 5 (7, 5, 5, 5) RS rows—44 (49,

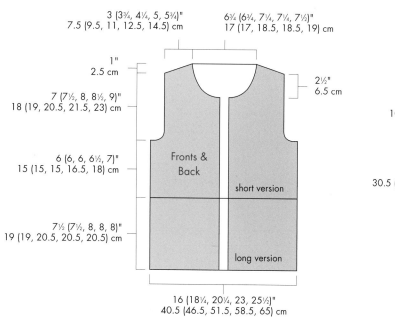

3 (3¾, 4¼, 5, 5¾)"
7.5 (9.5, 11, 12.5, 14.5) cm

6¾ (6¾, 7¼, 7¼, 7½)"
17 (17, 18.5, 18.5, 19) cm

1"
2.5 cm

2½"
6.5 cm

7 (7½, 8, 8½, 9)"
18 (19, 20.5, 21.5, 23) cm

Fronts & Back

6 (6, 6, 6½, 7)"
15 (15, 15, 16.5, 18) cm

short version

7½ (7½, 8, 8, 8)"
19 (19, 20.5, 20.5, 20.5) cm

long version

16 (18¼, 20¼, 23, 25½)"
40.5 (46.5, 51.5, 58.5, 65) cm

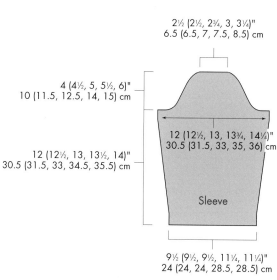

2½ (2½, 2¾, 3, 3¼)"
6.5 (6.5, 7, 7.5, 8.5) cm

4 (4½, 5, 5½, 6)"
10 (11.5, 12.5, 14, 15) cm

12 (12½, 13, 13¾, 14¼)"
30.5 (31.5, 33, 35, 36) cm

12 (12½, 13, 13½, 14)"
30.5 (31.5, 33, 34.5, 35.5) cm

Sleeve

9½ (9½, 9½, 11¼, 11¼)"
24 (24, 24, 28.5, 28.5) cm

Back

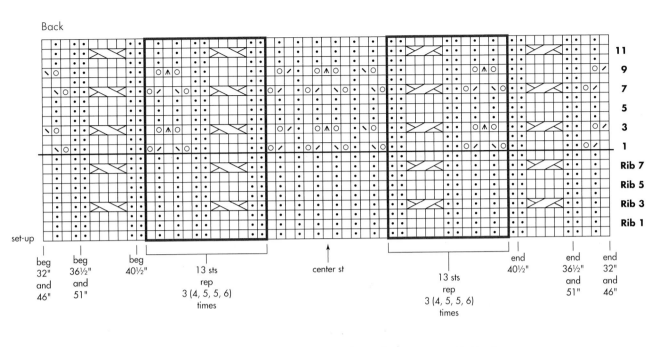

Rows (right side, top to bottom): 11, 9, 7, 5, 3, 1, Rib 7, Rib 5, Rib 3, Rib 1

set-up

beg 32" and 46" | beg 36½" and 51" | beg 40½" | 13 sts rep 3 (4, 5, 5, 6) times | center st | 13 sts rep 3 (4, 5, 5, 6) times | end 40½" | end 36½" and 51" | end 32" and 46"

☐	k on RS; p on WS
•	p on RS; k on WS
O	yo
/	k2tog
\	ssk
⋀	sl 2 sts as if to k2tog, k1, p2sso
2/2 LC	Sl 2 sts onto cn and hold in front, k2, k2 from cn.
2/2 RC	Sl 2 sts onto cn and hold in back, k2, k2 from cn.
☐ (bold)	pattern repeat

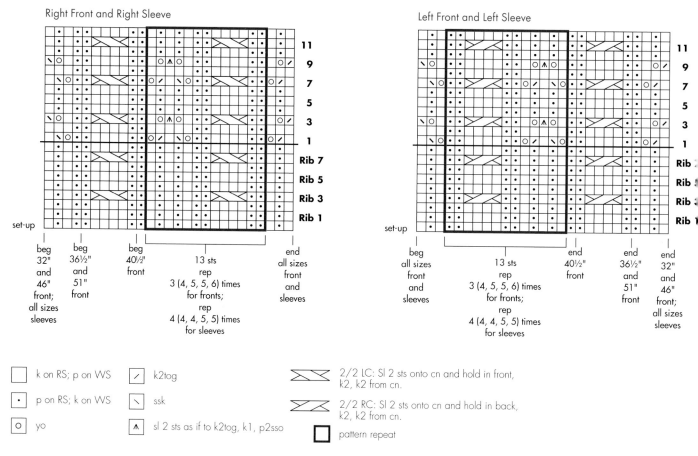

Right Front and Right Sleeve

Left Front and Left Sleeve

11 9 7 5 3 1
Rib 7 Rib 5 Rib 3 Rib 1

set-up

beg 32" and 46" front; all sizes sleeves

beg 36½" and 51" front

beg 40½" front

13 sts rep 3 (4, 5, 5, 6) times for fronts; rep 4 (4, 4, 5, 5) times for sleeves

end all sizes front and sleeves

set-up

beg all sizes front and sleeves

13 sts rep 3 (4, 5, 5, 6) times for fronts; rep 4 (4, 4, 5, 5) times for sleeves

end 40½" front

end 36½" and 51" front

end 32" and 46" front; all sizes sleeves

☐ k on RS; p on WS	╱ k2tog
• p on RS; k on WS	╲ ssk
◯ yo	⋏ sl 2 sts as if to k2tog, k1, p2sso

⟋⟍ 2/2 LC: Sl 2 sts onto cn and hold in front, k2, k2 from cn.

⟍⟋ 2/2 RC: Sl 2 sts onto cn and hold in back, k2, k2 from cn.

☐ pattern repeat

54, 61, 67) sts rem. Cont in patt as established until armhole measures 4½ (5, 5½, 6, 6½)" (11.5 [12.5, 14, 15, 16.5] cm), ending with a WS row.

Shape Neck

Keeping in patt, at neck edge (beg of RS rows) BO 7 (7, 8, 8, 9) sts once, then BO 3 sts once, then BO 2 sts 4 (4, 5, 5, 5) times—26 (31, 33, 40, 45) sts rem. Dec 1 st at beg of next 4 (4, 3, 3, 3) RS rows—22 (27, 30, 37, 42) sts rem. Cont even in patt until armhole measures same as back to beg of shoulder shaping, ending with a RS row.

Shape Shoulders

Keeping in patt, BO 5 (7, 7, 9, 10) sts at beg of next 2 WS rows, then BO 6 (7, 8, 9, 11) sts at beg of foll WS row, then BO 6 (6, 8, 10, 11) sts at beg of foll WS row—no sts rem.

LEFT FRONT

With smaller needles, CO 55 (64, 71, 81, 90) sts. *Set-up row:* (WS) K1 (selvedge st; knit every row), beg and ending as indicated for your size work, set-up row of Left Front and Left

The classic combination of lace and cables is always in style.

Sleeve chart over center 53 (62, 69, 79, 88) sts, k1 (selvedge st; knit every row). Knitting selvedge sts every row, work through WS Rib Row 8 of chart. Change to larger needles. *Next row:* (RS) Rep Rows 1–12 of Left Front and Left Sleeve chart (*do not* rep set-up or rib rows) until piece measures 6 (6, 6, 6½, 7)" (15 [15, 15, 16.5, 18] cm) from CO for short version or 13½ (13½, 14, 14½, 15)" (34.5 [34.5, 35.5, 37, 38] cm) from CO for long version, ending with a WS row.

Shape Armhole

BO 6 (8, 8, 9, 10) sts at beg of next RS row—49 (56, 63, 72, 80) sts rem. BO 2 sts at beg of next 0 (0, 2, 3, 4) RS rows, then dec 1 st at beg of next 5 (7, 5, 5, 5) RS rows—44 (49, 54, 61, 67) sts rem. Cont in patt as established until armhole measures 4½ (5, 5½, 6, 6½)" (11.5 [12.5, 14, 15, 16.5] cm), ending with a RS row.

Shape Neck

Keeping in patt, at neck edge (beg of WS rows) BO 7 (7, 8, 8, 9) sts once, then BO 3 sts once, then BO 2 sts 4 (4, 5, 5, 5) times—26 (31, 33, 40, 45) sts rem. Dec 1 st at end of next 4 (4, 3, 3, 3) RS rows—22 (27, 30, 37, 42) sts rem. Cont even in patt until armhole measures same as back to beg of shoulder shaping, ending with a WS row.

Shape Shoulders

Keeping in patt, BO 5 (7, 7, 9, 10) sts at beg of next 2 RS rows, then BO 6 (7, 8, 9, 11) sts at beg of foll RS row, then BO 6 (6, 8, 10, 11) sts at beg of foll RS row—no sts rem.

RIGHT SLEEVE

With smaller needles, CO 68 (68, 68, 81, 81) sts. *Set-up row:* (WS) K1 (selvedge st; knit every row), beg and ending as indicated for sleeves, work set-up row of Right Front and Sleeve chart over center 66 (66, 66, 79, 79) sts, k1 (selvedge st; knit every row). Knitting selvedge sts every row, work through WS Rib Row 8 of chart. Change to larger needles. *Next row:* (RS) Rep Rows 1–12 of Right Front and Right Sleeve chart (*do not* rep set-up or rib rows), and *at the same time* inc 1 st each end of needle every 6th row 0 (0, 6, 0, 0) times, then every 8th row 8 (11, 7, 0, 5) times, then every 10th row 2 (0, 0, 6, 6) times, then every 12th row 0 (0, 0, 3, 0) times, working new sts into established patt—88 (90, 94, 99, 103) sts. Work even in patt until piece measures 12 (12½, 13, 13½, 14)" (30.5 [31.5, 33, 34.5, 35.5] cm) from CO, ending with a WS row.

Shape Cap

BO 6 (8, 8, 9, 10) sts at beg of next 2 rows, then BO 2 sts at beg of next 0 (0, 4, 6, 8) rows—76 (74, 70, 69, 67) sts rem. Dec 1 st each end of needle every RS row 7 (11, 15, 17, 19) times—62 (52, 40, 35, 29) sts rem. BO 2 sts at beg of next 12 (10, 0, 0, 0) rows, then BO 3 sts at beg of next 4 (2, 4, 2, 2) rows, then BO 4 sts at beg of next 2 (2, 2, 2, 0) rows—18 (18, 20, 21, 23) sts rem. BO all sts.

LEFT SLEEVE

Work as for right sleeve, substituting Left Front and Sleeve chart.

FINISHING

With yarn threaded on a tapestry needle, sew shoulder seams.

Neckband

With smaller needles, RS facing, and beg at center right front, pick up and knit 7 (7, 8, 8, 9) sts along BO section of right front neck, 20 sts along shaped neck edge, 48 (48, 53, 53, 58) sts across back neck, 20 sts along shaped neck edge, and 7 (7, 8, 8, 9) sts along BO section of left front neck—102 (102, 109, 109, 116) sts total. Work as foll:

Row 1: (WS) K1 (selvedge st; knit every row), *k2, [p1, k1] 2 times, p1; rep from * to last 3 sts, k2, k1 (selvedge st; knit every row).

Row 2: K1 (selvedge st), *p2, [k1, p1] 2 times, k1; rep from * to last 3 sts, p2, k1 (selvedge st). Rep Rows 1 and 2 until neckband measures 1" (2.5 cm) from pick-up row. Loosely BO all sts in patt.

Buttonband

With RS of left front edge facing and beg at BO edge of neckband, pick up and knit 81 (81, 81, 88, 88) sts for short version or 123 (123, 123, 130, 130) sts for long version. Work in rib patt as for neckband for 9 rows. Loosely BO all sts patt. Mark position of 7 (7, 7, 8, 8) buttons for short version or 11 (11, 11, 12, 12) buttons for long version, evenly spaced along buttonband.

Buttonhole Band

With RS of right front edge facing and beg at CO edge of right front, pick up and knit 81 (81, 88, 88) sts for short version, or 123 (123, 123, 130, 130) sts for long version. Work in rib patt as for neckband for 3 rows. *Buttonhole row:* (RS) Cont in patt, work (yo twice, k2tog) buttonholes opposite each marked button position on buttonband. *Next row:* Work in patt, dropping extra wrap of each yo in previous row to maintain original stitch count. *Next row:* *Work in patt to buttonhole of previous row, insert needle tip into hole either kwise or pwise as required by the rib patt, and work 1 st in buttonhole; rep from * until last buttonhole has been worked, work in patt to end of row. Work 3 rows even in patt. Loosely BO all sts in patt.

With yarn threaded on tapestry needle, sew sleeve caps into armholes, matching shaping. Sew sleeve and side seams. Weave in loose ends. Sew buttons onto buttonband, opposite buttonholes. Lightly block to measurements.

Simultaneously elegant and whimsical, **Lois S. Young's** over-the-elbow fingerless gloves accessorize any sleeveless top or dress. The gloves begin at the upper arm with an edging pattern worked back and forth in rows until the circumference of the arm is reached. Stitches are then picked up along the straight edge of this strip, joined for working in the round, and worked downward to the fingers in alternating panels of stockinette and faggot stitch. A few crystals look like tiny buttons on the upper edging.

STITCH GUIDE

Wide Lace: (multiple of 8 sts)
Rnd 1: *K5, yo, k2tog, k1; rep from * to end of rnd.
Rnd 2: *K6, ssk, yo; rep from * to end of rnd.
Repeat Rnds 1 and 2 for pattern.

Medium Lace: (multiple of 7 sts)
Rnd 1: *K4, yo, k2tog; k1; rep from * to end of rnd.
Rnd 2: *K5, ssk, yo; rep from * to end of rnd.
Repeat Rnds 1 and 2 for pattern.

Narrow Lace: (multiple of 6 sts)
Rnd 1: *K3, yo, k2tog, k1; rep from * to end of rnd.
Rnd 2: *K4, ssk, yo; rep from * to end of rnd.
Repeat Rnds 1 and 2 for pattern.

NOTES
❖ Both gloves are worked the same and can be worn on either hand.
❖ Be careful that you do not accidentally drop any yarnover that occurs at the end of a needle or the end of a round.
❖ Work double yarnovers as purl 1, knit 1 on subsequent rows.
❖ Tie a piece of thread or place a removable marker in the first yarnover of the round following a decrease round to make it easier to measure the length between decrease rounds.

FINISHED SIZE
About 6" (15 cm) hand circumference, 9" (23 cm) elbow circumference with lace pattern relaxed, and 18" (45.5 cm) long. Gloves will stretch up to 2" (5 cm) more in circumference to accommodate a range of sizes.

YARN
Fingering weight (CYCA #1 Super Fine).
Shown here: Alchemy Yarns of Transformation Monarch (70% cashmere, 30% silk; 156 yd [142 m]/40 g): #044f cherry tart, 2 skeins.

NEEDLES
Size 2 (2.75 mm): set of 4 double-pointed (dpn). Adjust needle size if necessary to obtain the correct gauge.

NOTIONS
Markers (m); stitch holder; ten 4 mm beads; sewing needle and matching thread for attaching beads; piece of stiff paper or thin cardboard about 11 × 17" (28 × 43 cm) for blocking form.

GAUGE
28 stitches and 40 rounds = 4" (10) in wide lace pattern; lace edging pattern from chart measures 2½" (6.5 cm) wide at deepest point.

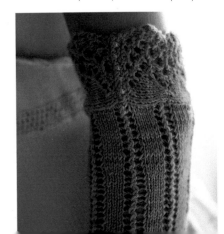

GLOVE

Lace Edging

CO 14 sts. Working back and forth in rows, knit 4 rows for bead placket. Change to Lace Edging chart and work Rows 1–12 a total of 7 times. Knit 5 rows for bead placket, beg and ending with a RS row—piece should measure about 9" (23 cm) from CO. With WS facing, BO all sts kwise.

Arm

Bring the CO and BO ends of the lace edging tog, overlap one garter bead placket on top of the other, and pin in place. *Note:* When making the second glove, pin the overlap with the opposite end on top so the finished plackets will be mirror images of one another. Join yarn with RS facing to straight selvedge of lace edging at beg of overlapped section. With RS facing, pick up and knit 1 st through both layers at overlap, then pick up and knit 55 more sts evenly spaced along straight selvedge so that every 8th picked-up st is aligned above a point in the lace zigzags of the edging—56 sts total. Place marker (pm) and join for working in the rnd. Work wide lace patt (see Stitch Guide) until piece measures 2" (5 cm) from pick-up rnd, ending with Rnd 2 of patt. *Next rnd:* *K2, ssk, k1, yo, k2tog, k1; rep from * to end—49 sts rem. Beg with Rnd 2 and marking the first yo of the rnd (see Notes), work medium lace patt (see Stitch Guide) until piece measures 4" (10 cm) from marker at start of medium lace patt, ending with Rnd 2 of patt. *Next rnd:* *K1, k2tog, k1, yo, k2tog, k1; rep from * to end—42 sts rem. Beg with Rnd 2 and marking the first yo of rnd, work narrow lace patt (see Stitch Guide) until piece measures 4¼" (11 cm) from marker at start of narrow lace patt, ending with Rnd 2 of patt—piece measures about 10¼" (26 cm) total from pick-up rnd.

Thumb Gusset

Cont in narrow lace patt as established, work 18 sts in patt, k1, pm, yo, k1, yo, pm, k1, work in patt to end of rnd—44 sts; 3 sts between gusset markers. Work 3 rnds even in patt, work-ing gusset sts between m in St st. *Gusset inc rnd:* Work in patt to first gusset m, sl m, yo, knit to next gusset m, yo, sl m, work in patt to end of rnd—2 sts inc'd between gusset m. Cont in patt as established, rep the shaping of the last 4 rnds 5 more times—56 sts total; 15 sts between gusset markers. Work 2 rnds even in patt. *Next rnd:* Keeping in patt, work to 1 st before first gusset m, place the next 17 sts on holder for thumb (remove gusset markers as you come to them), use the backward loop method (see Glossary, page 152) to CO 3 sts over thumb gap, work in patt to end—42 sts rem.

Hand

Cont even in patt until piece measures about 2" (5 cm) from sts CO above thumb gap. [Knit 1 rnd, purl 1 rnd] 2 times—piece measures about 15½" (39.5 cm) from pick-up rnd and 18" (45.5 cm) from widest point of lace edging. Loosely BO all sts pwise.

Thumb

Return 17 held thumb sts to 3 dpn so that there are 7 sts each on the first 2 needles and 3 sts on the third needle. With RS facing, join yarn to beg of first needle, knit across all 17 sts, then with the third needle pick up and knit 3 sts from base of sts CO over thumb gap—20 sts total; 7 sts each on the first 2 needles and 6 sts on the third needle. Pm and join for working in the rnd. [Knit 1 rnd, purl 1 rnd] 2 times, knit 1 rnd. Loosely BO all sts pwise.

FINISHING

With sewing needle and thread, sew 5 beads evenly spaced through both layers of bead placket to resemble a vertical line of tiny buttons. Weave in loose ends. To make a pair of blocking forms, trace your arm and hand with slightly outspread fingers twice onto a piece of heavy paper or cardboard. Cut out both forms along the tracing lines. Insert forms into gloves. Spritz with water and lay flat, pinning out the points of lace edging. Allow to thoroughly air-dry. Turn gloves over with forms still in place and spritz and block other side of each glove in the same manner.

Lace Edging

k on RS; p on WS

· p on RS; k on WS

o yo

/ k2tog on RS; p2tog on WS

\ ssk on RS; ssp on WS

Stack yarnovers and decreases on top of each other for a strong vertical pattern.

For the most part, lace patterns do not make insulating fabric and are rarely considered appropriate for warm winter hats. But by layering a decorative lace pattern over dense stockinette stitch, **Mona Schmidt** found a way to make this hat both lacy and warm. Mona worked the layers in contrasting but coordinating colors—orange and red—and experimented with lace patterns until she found one with plenty of large eyelets to reveal the solid layer underneath.

STITCH GUIDE

Knit into Back, Purl into Front Increase (k1b-p1f inc): Knit into the back of next st, then purl into the front of same st, and slip st from needle—1 st inc'd; 2 sts made from 1 st.

Sssk: Slip 3 sts individually kwise, insert left needle tip into the fronts of these 3 sts, and use the right needle to knit them tog through their back loops.

NOTES

❖ The hat is worked in the round beginning at the top of the crown for the stockinette lining, and worked downward to the knit-and-purl textured brim. The lace outer layer is worked upwards from the textured brim to the top of the crown.

❖ When working the brim and lace outer layer, the wrong (purl) side of the lining will be on the outside of the work. This allows the right (knit) side of the lining to show through the lace fabric when the stockinette lining is tucked inside the finished hat.

❖ Some rounds of the lace pattern have yarnovers at the beginning and end of the round. For these rounds you may find it helpful to make the final yarnover, and then immediately work the first stitch of the next rnd (the yarnover from the beginning of the round), in order to avoid accidentally dropping one of the yarnovers.

❖ Pay close attention to any double yarnovers in the lace pattern to make sure that you work each double yarnover as p1, k1 on the following even-numbered round as shown on chart, and do not accidentally drop one of the yarnover loops.

FINISHED SIZE

About 19½" (49.5 cm) head circumference and 8¼" (21 cm) tall, after blocking. Will stretch to fit up to 23" (58.5 cm) head circumference.

YARN

Sportweight (CYCA #2 Fine).

Shown here: Reynolds Soft Sea Wool (100% wool; 162 yd [148 m]/50 g): #853 orange (MC) and #969 red (CC), 1 ball each.

NEEDLES

Lining and brim—size 2 (2.75 mm): set of 4 or 5 double-pointed (dpn) and 16" (40 cm) circular (cir). Lace outer layer—size 4 (3.5 mm): set of 4 or 5 dpn and 16" (40 cm) cir. Adjust needle size if necessary to obtain the correct gauge.

NOTIONS

Markers (m); tapestry needle.

GAUGE

13 sts and 23 rnds = 2" (5 cm) in St st on smaller needles worked in the round, after blocking.

Layer an openwork
pattern over a solid
fabric to gain warmth
and unexpected color.

LINING

With orange and smaller dpn, CO 6 sts. Arrange sts evenly on 3 dpn (2 sts each needle) place marker (pm), and join for working in the rnd, being careful not to twist sts. Knit 1 rnd.

Rnd 1: *K1b-p1f inc (see Stitch Guide); rep from * to end of rnd—12 sts; 4 sts on each needle.

Even-numbered Rnds 2–38: Knit.

Rnd 3: *K1; k1b-p1f inc; rep from * to end—18 sts; 6 sts on each needle.

Rnd 5: *K2, k1b-p1f inc; rep from * to end—24 sts; 8 sts on each needle.

Rnd 7: *K3, k1b-p1f inc; rep from * to end—30 sts; 10 sts on each needle.

Rnd 9: *K4, k1b-p1f inc; rep from * to end—36 sts; 12 sts on each needle.

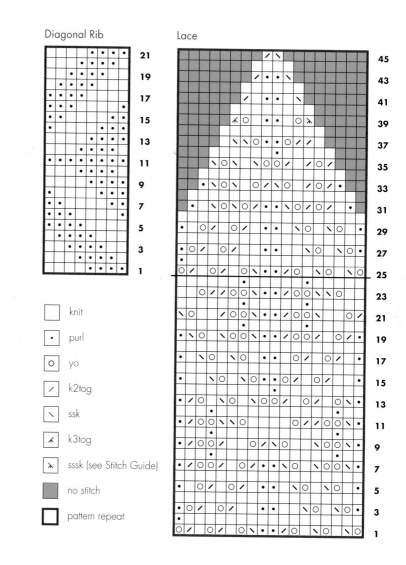

Diagonal Rib

Lace

knit
purl
yo
k2tog
ssk
k3tog
sssk (see Stitch Guide)
no stitch
pattern repeat

Rnd 11: *K5, k1b-p1f inc; rep from * to end—42 sts; 14 sts on each needle.

Odd-numbered Rnds 13–39: Cont in this manner, working 1 more st before the inc in every odd-numbered rnd until Rnd 39 has been completed, and changing to smaller cir when there are too many sts to fit on the dpn—126 sts.

Rnd 40: Knit.

Change to smaller cir needle if you have not already done so. Work even in St st until piece measures 4" (10 cm) from last inc rnd (about 45 rnds St st), and about 7½" (19 cm) from beg. Cut orange yarn, leaving an 8" (20.5 cm) tail.

BRIM

Push the lining through the center of the needle so the purl side of the lining is on the outside of the rnd (see Notes). With WS of lining facing you, join red yarn. *Next rnd:* (RS of brim; WS of lining) K19, k2tog; rep from * to end—120 sts. Work Rnds 1–21 of Diagonal Rib chart—brim measures about 1½" (3.8 cm), and piece measures about 9" (23 cm) from CO. Change to larger cir needle and knit 1 rnd. With smaller cir needle and knit side of lining facing, slip the smaller needle into each st of first red yarn rnd to pick up 120 sts; these sts are just picked up and placed on the needle without working them, not picked up and knit. Fold brim in half along the purled fold line from Rnd 11 of chart to bring the two needles tog with RS of brim facing outwards, and needle with picked-up lining sts in back of needle with live brim sts. Holding both needles tog in the left hand, *k2tog to join 1 brim st tog with 1 lining st; rep from * to end—still 120 sts.

LACE OUTER LAYER

Next rnd: *K2, k2tog; rep from * to end of rnd—90 sts rem. Change to Lace chart, and rep Rnds 1–24 of chart 2 times, then work Rnds 25–45 once, changing to larger dpn when there are too few sts to fit around the cir needle—10 sts rem; 69 lace patt rnds completed; piece measures about 8¼" (21 cm) from purled fold line of brim. Cut yarn, leaving an 8" (20.5 cm) tail. Thread tail on tapestry needle, draw through rem sts drawstring-fashion, pull tight to close top of crown. Tuck lining inside hat so St st side of lining shows through the openwork lace patt. Use tail from outer lace layer to stitch the center of both crowns tog, and fasten off on WS of hat.

FINISHING

Weave loose ends. Block to measurements.

Work double yarnovers for really big holes.

SHOW-OFF RUFFLE SKIRT
KAT COYLE

For this flirty knitted skirt, **Kat Coyle** worked the bobble lace ruffle back and forth in rows. She then joined the ruffle into a circle and worked a slimming twisted-rib pattern in the round to the waist. The ruffle's lacy pattern is made by intentionally dropping individual stitches and letting them ravel down to the cast-on edge. A silk ribbon tied into a bow at the back of the top of the ruffle gives the skirt a slight vintage touch.

STITCH GUIDE

Twisted Rib: (multiple of 4 sts)
All Rnds: *K1 through back loop (k1tbl), p3; rep from * to end of rnd.

Bobble (MB): Knit into the front, back, front, back, and front of same st—1 st inc'd to 5 sts. *Turn work, k5, turn, p5; rep from * once more, slip 2nd, 3rd, 4th, and 5th sts on right needle over first st, return rem st to left needle and knit this st through the back loop.

Bobble Lace: (multiple of 9 sts + 10)
Rows 1 and 3: (RS) *K1 through back loop (k1tbl), p2; rep from * to last st, sl 1 pwise with yarn in back (wyb).
Row 2 and all WS rows: P1 through back loop (p1tbl), *k1tbl, k1, p1tbl; rep from * to last 3 sts, k1tbl, k1, sl 1 pwise with yarn in front (wyf).

NOTES

❖ When the bobble lace pattern is viewed with the right side facing, the bobbles are made in the second stitch of each purl-2 column (except for the purl-2 columns closest to the selvedges, which do not have any bobbles). Take care to always make the bobble in the second of the two purl stitches because the first purl stitch will be dropped and raveled back to the cast-on edge later to form the lace.

❖ You may need to pull gently on the fabric to coax the dropped stitches to ravel down to the cast-on edge.

❖ The skirt is planned to be about 24" (61 cm) long below the waistband. To customize the length, work more or fewer rounds before beginning the decreases in the twisted rib section of the skirt. Every 7 rounds added or removed will lengthen or shorten the skirt by about 1" (2.5 cm).

FINISHED SIZE
37¾ (39¾, 42, 44¼, 46¼)" (96 [101, 106.5, 112.5, 117.5] cm) hip circumference measured about 8" (20.5 cm) below waistband, and 28¼ (30, 31¾, 33¼, 35)" (72 [76, 80.5, 84.5, 89] cm) waist circumference. Skirt shown measures 37¾" (96 cm) at hip.

YARN
Sportweight (CYCA #2 Fine).
Shown here: Classic Elite Princess (40% merino, 28% viscose, 15% nylon, 10% cashmere, 7% angora; 150 yd [137 m]/50 g): #3455 patrician port (dark red), 7 (7, 8, 8, 8) balls.

NEEDLES
Lower lace section—size 5 (3.75 mm): 24" (60 cm) circular (cir). Skirt body—size 6 (4 mm): 24" (60 cm) cir. Adjust needle size if necessary to obtain the correct gauge.

NOTIONS
Marker (m); tapestry needle; 54" (1.4 meter) of 1" (2.5 cm) wide silk ribbon.

GAUGE
About 15 stitches and 22 rows = 4" (10 cm) in bobble lace pattern on smaller needle, after blocking. 22 stitches and 29 rows = 4" (10 cm) in twisted rib pattern on larger needle, slightly stretched.

Row 5: (bobble row) K1tbl, p2, *[k1tbl, p2] 2 times, k1tbl, p1, MB (see Stitch Guide); rep from * to last 7 sts, [k1tbl, p2] 2 times, sl 1 wyb.

Rows 7, 9, and 11: Rep Row 1.

Row 13: (bobble row) K1tbl, p2, *k1tbl, p1, MB, [k1tbl, p2] 2 times; rep from * to last 7 sts, k1tbl, p1, MB, k1tbl, p2, sl 1 wyb.

Rows 15, 17, and 19: Rep Row 1.

Row 21: (bobble row) K1tbl, p2, *k1tbl, p2, k1tbl, p1, MB, k1tbl, p2; rep from * to last 7 sts, [k1tbl, p2] 2 times, sl 1 wyb.

Row 23: Rep Row 1.

Row 24: Rep Row 2.

Repeat Rows 1–24 for patt.

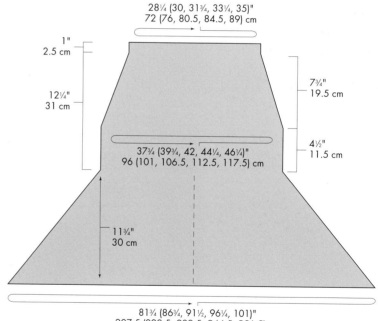

28¼ (30, 31¾, 33¼, 35)"
72 (76, 80.5, 84.5, 89) cm

1"
2.5 cm

12¼"
31 cm

7¾"
19.5 cm

37¾ (39¾, 42, 44¼, 46¼)"
96 (101, 106.5, 112.5, 117.5) cm

4½"
11.5 cm

11¾"
30 cm

81¾ (86¾, 91½, 96¼, 101)"
207.5 (220.5, 232.5, 244.5, 256.5) cm

SKIRT

With smaller size needle and using the long-tail method (see Glossary, page 153), firmly CO 307 (325, 343, 361, 379) sts. Do *not* join for working in the rnd. Work bobble lace patt (see Stitch Guide) back and forth in rows for 64 rows, ending with WS Row 16 of patt—8 bobble rows completed. *Drop st row:* (RS) K1tbl, p2, *k1tbl, drop next st off needle and let it ravel down to CO edge, p1; rep from * to last 4 sts, k1tbl, p3—207 (219, 231, 243, 255) sts rem. With RS of work still facing, change to larger needle, place marker (pm) to denote center back, and join for working in the rnd. *Inc rnd:* K1tbl, p1f&b (see Glossary, page 156), p1, *k1tbl, p3; rep from * to end—208 (220, 232, 244, 256) sts. Work in twisted rib (see Stitch Guide) for about 33 rnds, or until piece measures 4½" (11.5 cm) from beg of twisted rib patt. If adjusting length (see Notes), work more or fewer rnds here as desired.

Decrease for Waist

Dec Rnd 1: *[K1tbl, p3] 3 (4, 4, 4, 3) times, k1tbl, p1, p2tog; rep from * to last, 0 (0, 12, 4, 0) sts, work last 0 (0, 12, 4, 0) sts in est patt—13 (11, 11, 12, 16) p3 columns dec'd to p2; 195 (209, 221, 232, 240) sts rem.
Work 13 (10, 10, 10, 13) rnds even, working all single-st knit columns as k1tbl, and all purl columns as either p3 or p2 as they appear.

Dec Rnd 2: *[K1tbl, p3] 2 (3, 3, 3, 2) times, k1tbl, p1, p2tog, k1tbl, p2; rep from * to last, 0 (0, 12, 4, 0) sts, work last 0 (0, 12, 4, 0) sts in established patt—182 (198, 210, 220, 224) sts rem.

Work 13 (10, 10, 10, 13) rnds even.

Dec Rnd 3: *[K1tbl, p3] 1 (2, 2, 2, 1) time(s), k1tbl, p1, p2tog, [k1tbl, p2] 2 times; rep from * to last, 0 (0, 12, 4, 0) sts, [k1tbl, p3] 0 (0, 2, 0, 0) time(s), k1tbl, p1, p2tog 0 (0, 1, 1, 0) time— 169 (187, 198, 207, 208) sts rem.

Work 13 (10, 10, 10, 13) rnds even.

Dec Rnd 4: *[K1tbl, p3] 0 (1, 1, 1, 0) time, k1tbl, p1, p2tog, [k1tbl, p2] 3 times; rep from * to last, 0 (0, 11, 3, 0) sts, [k1tbl, p3] 0 (0, 2, 0, 0) time(s), k1tbl, p2 0 (0, 1, 1, 0) time—156 (176, 187, 195, 192) sts rem.

Work 13 (10, 10, 10, 13) rnds even.

Hip sizes (39¾, 42, 44¼)" only : Work 1 more dec rnd, working rem 11 (13, 12) p3 columns as p1, p2tog—165 (174, 183) sts rem. Work 11 (11, 11) rnds even.

All sizes: When all shaping has been completed there will be 156 (165, 174, 183, 192) sts; all p3 columns of starting twisted rib patt have been dec'd to p2 columns; about 90 rnds completed in twisted rib patt; piece measures about 24" (61 cm) from CO, or desired length to waistband.

Waistband

Work waistband with eyelets for draw-string as foll:

Rnd 1: Purl.

Rnds 2 and 3: Knit.

Rnd 4: *K1, yo, k2tog; rep from * to end.

Rnds 5 and 6: Knit.

BO all sts pwise.

FINISHING

Drawstring

With smaller needle, CO 236 (246, 257, 267, 278) sts. *Next row:* K2, MB (see Stitch Guide), [k5, MB] 2 times, knit to last 15 sts, [MB, k5] 2 times, MB, k2. BO all sts kwise.

Weave in all loose ends. Gently wet-block skirt to measurements, noting that the length will be slightly shorter at the back slit than at center front because of the slipped selvedge sts in the bobble lace section. Allow to air-dry completely. With yarn threaded on a tapestry needle, sew the top 4" (10 cm) of back slit closed, leaving lower part of slit open. Fold skirt in half with back slit along one fold line in order to identify center front at other fold line. Beg and ending with the eyelet as close as possible to center front, weave drawstring through eyelets in waistband. Beg and ending at center back, weave silk ribbon through top line of drop st openings just below start of twisted rib patt, and tie ends of ribbon into a bow at top of center back seam.

Intentionally dropped stitches create a lacy pattern.

Openwork zigs and zags give a ribbed appearance to **Lisa Daehlin's** casually dressy leg warmers. Ribbed edgings at top and bottom border a pattern that alternates fagot lace with panels of wavy stockinette stitch. To allow for the increased circumference of the calf, Lisa changed to larger needles along the way. Wear these leg warmers over brightly colored stockings for a bold, kicky look.

STITCH GUIDE

Lace Pattern: (multiple of 19 sts)

Rnd 1: *K2tog, k2, yo, k1, [yo, ssk] 3 times, yo, k2, k2tog, k4; rep from * to end of rnd.

Rnd 2: Knit to last st of rnd, sl last st to beg of first needle; slipped st becomes the first st of Rnd 3.

Rnd 3: *K2tog, k2, yo, k3, [yo, ssk] 3 times, yo, k2, k2tog, k2; rep from * to end of rnd.

Rnd 4: Knit to last st of rnd, sl last st to beg of first needle; slipped st becomes the first st of Rnd 5.

Rnd 5: *K2tog, k2, yo, k5, [yo, ssk] 3 times, yo, k2, k2tog; rep from * to end of rnd.

Rnd 6: Knit to last st of rnd, sl last st to beg of first needle; slipped st becomes the first st of Rnd 7.

Rnd 7: *K2tog, k4, k2tog, k2, [yo, k2tog] 3 times, yo, k1, yo, k2; rep from * to end of rnd.

Rnds 8 and 10: Knit.

Rnd 9: *[K2tog, k2] 2 times, [yo, k2tog] 3 times, yo, k3, yo, k2; rep from * to end of rnd.

Rnd 11: *[K2tog] 2 times, k2, [yo, k2tog] 3 times, yo, k5, yo, k2; rep from * to end of rnd.

Rnd 12: Knit.

Repeat Rnds 1–12 for pattern.

Increased Lace Pattern: (multiple of 19 sts, inc'd to multiple of 23 sts)

Rnd 1: *K2tog, k4, k2tog, k2, [yo, k2tog] 2 times, [yo, k1] 3 times, yo, k2; rep from * to end of rnd—patt has inc'd to a multiple of 21 sts.

Rnds 2, 4, and 6: Knit.

Rnd 3: *[K2tog, k2] 2 times, [yo, k2tog] 4 times, yo, k3, yo, k2; rep from * to end of rnd.

Rnd 5: *[K2tog] 2 times, k2, [yo, k2tog] 4 times, yo, k5, yo, k2; rep from * to end of rnd.

Rnd 7: *K2tog, k2, yo, k1, [yo, ssk] 4 times, yo, k2, k2tog, k4; rep from * to end of rnd.

Rnd 8: Knit to last st of rnd, sl last st to beg of first needle; slipped st becomes the first st of Rnd 9.

Rnd 9: *K2tog, k2, yo, k3, [yo, ssk] 4 times, yo, k2, k2tog, k2; rep from * to end of rnd.

FINISHED SIZE

About 15" (38 cm) thigh circumference and 23½" (59.5 cm) long, with fabric relaxed. Thigh circumference will stretch to about 19½" (49.5 cm) and length will stretch up to 26" (66 cm).

YARN

Fingering weight (CYCA #1 Super Fine).

Shown here: Filatura di Crosa Zarina (100% wool; 181 yd [165 m]/50 g): #1732 dark orange, 4 balls.

NEEDLES

Sizes 3, 4, and 5 (3.25, 3.5, and 3.75 cm): set of 5 double-pointed (dpn) for each size. Adjust needle size if necessary to obtain the correct gauge.

NOTIONS

Marker (m); tapestry needle.

GAUGE

26½ stitches and 43 rounds = 4" (10 cm) in lace pattern using smallest needles; 25½ stitches and 42 rounds = 4" (10 cm) in lace pattern using medium-size needles; 24½ stitches and 38 rounds = 4"(10 cm) in lace pattern using largest needles. All gauges are measured with fabric slightly stretched and gently patted to lie flat.

Rnd 10: Knit to last st of rnd, sl last st to beg of first needle; slipped st becomes the first st of Rnd 11.

Rnd 11: *K2tog, k2, yo, k5, [yo, ssk] 4 times, yo, k2, k2tog; rep from * to end of rnd.

Rnd 12: Knit to last st of rnd, sl last st to beg of first needle; slipped st becomes the first st of Rnd 13.

Rnd 13: *K2tog, k4, k2tog, k2, [yo, k2tog] 3 times, [yo, k1] 3 times, yo, k2—patt has inc'd to a multiple of 23 sts.

Rnds 14, 16, and 18: Knit.

Rnd 15: *[K2tog, k2] 2 times, [yo, k2tog] 5 times, yo, k3, yo, k2; rep from * to end of rnd.

Rnd 17: *[K2tog] 2 times, k2, [yo, k2tog] 5 times, yo, k5, yo, k2; rep from * to end of rnd.

Rnd 19: *K2tog, k2, yo, k1, [yo, ssk] 5 times, yo, k2, k2tog, k4; rep from * to end of rnd.

Rnd 20: Knit to last st of rnd, sl last st to beg of first needle; slipped st becomes the first st of Rnd 21.

Rnd 21: *K2tog, k2, yo, k3, [yo, ssk] 5 times, yo, k2, k2tog, k2; rep from * to end of rnd.

Rnd 22: Knit to last st of rnd, sl last st to beg of first needle; slipped st becomes the first st of Rnd 23.

Rnd 23: *K2tog, k2, yo, k5, [yo, ssk] 5 times, yo, k2, k2tog; rep from * to end of rnd.

Rnd 24: Knit.

LEG COZY

With smallest needles, CO 76 sts. Divide sts evenly on 4 dpn (19 sts each needle), place marker (pm), and join for working in the rnd, being careful not to twist sts. Work in k2, p2 rib until piece measures 3½" (9 cm) from CO. Beg with Rnd 1, rep Rnds 1–12 of lace patt (see Stitch Guide) 9 times—108 patt rnds completed; piece measures about 13½" (34.5 cm) from CO. Change to middle-size needles and rep Rnds 1–12 three more times—144 patt rnds completed; piece measures about 17" (43 cm) from CO. Change to largest needles and work Rnds 1–12 once, then work Rnds 1–6 once more, remembering to sl last st of Rnd 6 to beg of first needle as required by patt—162 patt rnds completed; piece measures about 19" (48.5 cm) from CO. Redistribute sts so there are 19 sts on each needle, making sure that the slipped st from the end of Rnd 6 stays in position as the first st of the rnd. Change to increased lace patt (see Stitch Guide) and work Rnds 1–24 once—84 sts after completing Rnd 1; 92 sts after completing Rnd 13; piece measures about 21½" (54.5 cm) from CO. Change to smallest needles and work in k2, p2 rib for 2" (5 cm)—piece measures about 23½" (59.5 cm) from CO. BO all sts very loosely in patt; top edge must be able to stretch to about 19½" (49.5 cm) circumference. Make another the same.

FINISHING

Weave in loose ends.

Shifting the arrangement of decreases and yarnovers creates a pattern that zigs and zags.

You'll often see lace used as panels or insertions in otherwise plain garments. Typically, the insertions are simple vertical or horizontal strips of lace. But in this striking sweater, **Norah Gaughan** carved out a broad notch at the front neckline and filled it with an asymmetrical lace motif that forms scalloping ripples at the neck. The openwork pattern in the neck insert is repeated as an allover pattern in the sleeves. When worn, the intentionally narrow sleeves stretch slightly to showcase the lacy look.

> **TIP**
> After the lace pattern has been established on the first row, the second stitch of the two stitches purled together will always be a yarnover.

STITCH GUIDE

Lace Pattern: (even number of sts)
All rows: *Yo, p2tog; rep from * to end of row.

Right Cross with Yarnover (RC with yo): Sl 2 sts onto cn and hold in back, k3, (yo, p2tog) from cn.

Left Cross with Yarnover (LC with yo): Sl 3 sts to cn and hold in front, yo, p2tog, k3 from cn.

BACK

With smaller needles, CO 102 (114, 126, 138) sts. *Next row:* (WS) P2, k2; rep from * to last 2 sts, p2. Cont in k2, p2 rib as established until piece measures 1½" (3.8 cm) from CO, ending with a WS row and dec 2 sts on last row—100 (112, 124, 136) sts rem. Change to larger needles and St st. Work even until piece measures 14" (35.5 cm) from CO, ending with a RS row.

Shape Armholes

BO 4 sts at beg of next 2 (2, 4, 4) rows, then BO 3 sts at beg of the foll 2 (4, 4, 6) rows, then BO 2 sts at beg of foll 4 rows—78 (84, 88, 94) sts rem. Work 1 WS row even. *Next row:* K2, k2tog, knit to last 4 sts, ssk, k2—2 sts dec'd. Dec 1 st each end of needle in this manner on the next 2 (2, 1, 1) RS row(s)—72 (78, 84, 90) sts rem. Cont even until armholes measure 7 (7½, 8, 8½)" (18 [19, 20.5, 21.5] cm), ending with a WS row.

FINISHED SIZE
36 (40½, 45, 49½)" (91.5 [103, 114.5, 125.5] cm) bust circumference. Sweater shown measures 36" (91.5 cm).

YARN
DK weight (CYCA #3 Light).
Shown here: Berroco Softwist (59% rayon, 41% wool; 100 yd [91 m]/50 g): #9410 semi-sweet (chocolate brown), 10 (12, 13, 15) hanks.

NEEDLES
Body and sleeves—size 6 (4 mm). Ribbing—size 4 (3.5 mm). Adjust needle size if necessary to obtain the correct gauge.

NOTIONS
Cable needle (cn); removable marker; stitch holder (optional); tapestry needle; size G/6 (4 mm) crochet hook;

GAUGE
22 stitches and 30 rows = 4" (10 cm) in stockinette stitch on larger needles; 16 stitches and 40 rows = 4" (10 cm) in lace pattern on larger needles before blocking.

Shape Neck

(RS) K19 (22, 25, 28), join new yarn and BO center 34 sts, knit to end—19 (22, 25, 28) sts rem each side. Working each side separately, at each neck edge BO 5 sts 2 times—9 (12, 15, 18) sts rem. Cont even until armholes measure 8 (8½, 9, 9½)" (20.5 [21.5, 23, 24] cm), ending with a WS row. With RS facing, BO all sts.

FRONT

CO and work as for back until piece measures 14" (35.5 cm) from CO, ending with a RS row.

Shape Armholes and Neck

Note: Front neck shaping starts while armhole shaping is in progress; read the next sections all the way through before proceeding so you do not accidentally work past the point where neck shaping begins. Work armhole shaping as for back until 14 (17, 20, 23) sts have been removed at each side by armhole shaping. *At the same time,* beg neck shaping when piece measures 14 (14½, 15, 15½)" (35.5 [37, 38, 39.5] cm) from CO and armholes measure 0 (½, 1, 1½)" (0 [1.3, 2.5, 3.8] cm); for size 36", the neck shaping will begin on the first RS row of the armhole shaping. Place a marker in the center of the sts on the needle for center front. On the first RS row

Lace sleeves dress up any sweater.

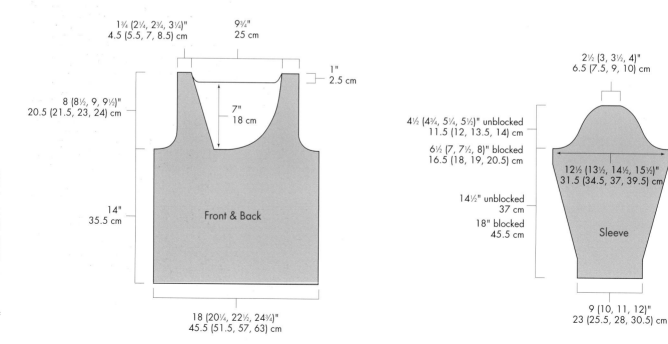

1¾ (2¼, 2¾, 3¼)"
4.5 (5.5, 7, 8.5) cm

9¾"
25 cm

1"
2.5 cm

8 (8½, 9, 9½)"
20.5 (21.5, 23, 24) cm

7"
18 cm

14"
35.5 cm

Front & Back

18 (20¼, 22½, 24¾)"
45.5 (51.5, 57, 63) cm

2½ (3, 3½, 4)"
6.5 (7.5, 9, 10) cm

4½ (4¾, 5¼, 5½)" unblocked
11.5 (12, 13.5, 14) cm

6½ (7, 7½, 8)" blocked
16.5 (18, 19, 20.5) cm

12½ (13½, 14½, 15½)"
31.5 (34.5, 37, 39.5) cm

14½" unblocked
37 cm

18" blocked
45.5 cm

Sleeve

9 (10, 11, 12)"
23 (25.5, 28, 30.5) cm

of neck shaping, knit to 1 st past center m for left front neck, place sts just worked on a holder if desired (optional), join new ball of yarn and BO 12 sts, knit to end for right front neck.

Right front neck: Working on sts of right front neck only, cont required armhole shaping and *at the same time* dec 1 st at neck edge every 4th row 14 times as foll: On RS rows, k2, k2tog, knit to end including any armhole shaping; on WS rows, purl to last 4 sts including any armhole shaping, p2tog, p2—9 (12, 15, 18) sts rem when neck and armhole shaping is completed. Work even until armhole measures 8 (8½, 9, 9½)" (20.5 [21.5, 23, 24] cm), ending with a WS row. With RS facing, BO sts for right front shoulder.

Left front neck: If you placed sts of left front neck on holder, return them to larger straight needles. Rejoin yarn with WS facing. Cont required armhole shaping and *at the same time*, at neck edge (beg of WS rows), BO 4 sts once, then BO 3 sts 2 times, then BO 2 sts 5 times—20 sts removed from neck. Cont armhole shaping as necessary, dec 1 st at neck edge every RS row 4 times, then every other RS row 4 times as foll: Knit to last 4 sts including any armhole shaping, ssk, k2—9 (12, 15, 18) sts rem when all neck and armhole shaping is complete. Work even until armhole measures 8 (8½, 9, 9½)" (20.5 [21.5, 23, 24] cm), ending with a WS row. With RS facing, BO all sts.

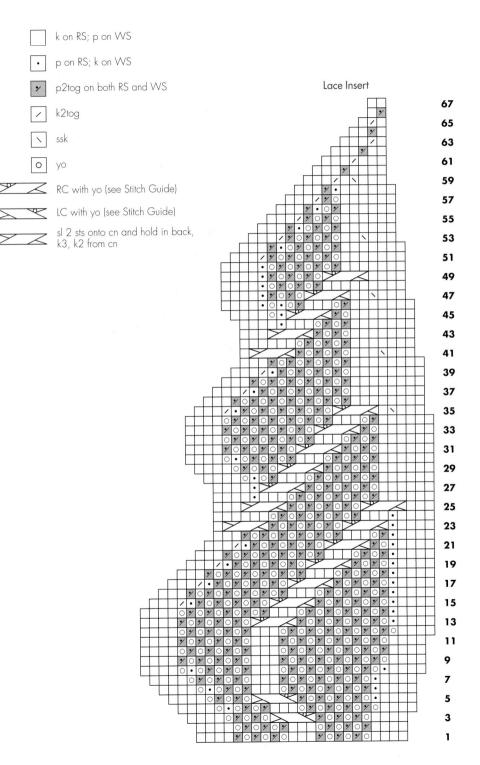

Lace Insert

□	k on RS; p on WS
·	p on RS; k on WS
⊻	p2tog on both RS and WS
/	k2tog
\	ssk
o	yo
⧖	RC with yo (see Stitch Guide)
⧖	LC with yo (see Stitch Guide)
⧖	sl 2 sts onto cn and hold in back, k3, k2 from cn

SLEEVES

With smaller needles, CO 38 (42, 46, 50) sts. Work in k2, p2 rib as for back until piece measures 2" (5 cm) from CO, ending with a WS row and dec 2 sts evenly spaced on last row—36 (40, 44, 48) sts rem. Change to larger needles and establish patts on next row as foll: (RS) K2 (edge sts), work lace patt (see Stitch Guide) to last 2 sts, k2 (edge sts). Keeping 2 sts at each side in St st as established, cont in lace patt, inc 1 st each end of needle just inside the edge sts every 14th row 7 times, working new sts into patt—50 (54, 58, 62) sts. *Note:* When shaping sleeve, wait until you have 2 new sts at each side before working the new sts into patt; on rows where there is only 1 new st at each side, work the new sts in St st as for edge sts. Cont even as established until piece measures 14½" (37 cm) from CO with fabric relaxed; sleeve will measure about 18" (45.5 cm) long from CO after blocking.

Shape Cap

BO 3 sts at beg of the next 2 rows, then BO 2 sts at beg of foll 2 rows—40 (44, 48, 52) sts rem. Dec 1 st each end of needle on next RS row, then every 4th row 8 (9, 10, 11) times, then on next RS row once—20 (22, 24, 26) sts rem. BO 2 sts at beg of next 2 rows, then BO 3 sts at beg of foll 2 rows—10 (12, 14, 16) sts rem; cap measures about 4½ (4¾, 5¼, 5½)" (11.5 [12, 13.5, 14] cm); cap will measure about 6½ (7, 7½, 8)" (16.5 [18, 19, 20.5] cm) after blocking. With RS facing, BO all sts.

LACE INSERT

With larger needles, CO 23 sts. Beg with Row 1, work through Row 67 of Lace Insert chart—2 sts rem. BO all sts.

FINISHING

Block pieces to finished measurements shown on schematic. Block lace insert lightly; allow St st along scalloped edge to roll slightly to WS. With yarn threaded on a tapestry needle, sew lace insert to front neck opening with the CO edge of the insert against the right front neck and the smoother selvedge of the insert against the curve of the left front neck; scalloped edge of insert will be at top of neck. Sew shoulder seams. Sew sleeve caps into armholes, then sew sleeve and side seams.

Neck Edging

Join yarn to right front neck at top edge of lace insert. With RS facing and using a crochet hook, work 1 row of slip stitch crochet (see Glossary, page 154, for crochet instructions) around rem neck opening, ending at top edge of lace insert on left front; do not crochet along the scalloped edge of insert. With RS still facing, work 1 row of rev sc around neck opening, ending where you began at top edge of lace insert on right front. Fasten off last st. Weave in loose ends.

From simple to complex, lace patterns can be worked as inserts in otherwise plain garments.

GRETA GARBO GARDEN HAT

ANNIE MODESITT

There was a time when a well-dressed lady never left the house without a hat. For those days when a wide-brimmed hat is still in order, **Annie Modesitt** has designed a knitted version of this elegant staple. The lacy crown and brim on this not-so-basic black hat are knitted with merino yarn and trimmed with a chenille yarn that looks like velvet. Annie uses traditional milliner's techniques of blocking and wiring to shape the hat. Wear this hat to a garden party or to tour the countryside in a classy convertible.

STITCH GUIDE

Picot Bind-Off: *Using knitting needles:* *Ssk, return st on right needle to left needle and knit this st again, return st to left needle; rep from * to end. *Using a crochet hook:* (see Glossary, page 154, for crochet instructions) Sl next 2 sts to crochet hook as if to knit, *yo hook and draw through both sts on hook, ch 1, sl next st to crochet hook as if to knit; rep from *. For both methods, when 1 st rem, cut yarn, draw tail through last st to fasten off.

NOTES

❖ To reproduce the wired and blocked gauge of the hat without having to wire your swatch, cast on about 30 sts and work in stockinette stitch for a little more than 4" (10 cm). Bind off all stitches. Press the swatch with an iron, pulling it tautly in both directions. Allow swatch to cool, then measure for gauge.

❖ The headsize is the part of the hat that sits just above the ears. The headsize is generally the circumference of the head (measured just at the top of the ears) plus ½–1" (1.3–2.5 cm), depending on fit of the hat.

FINISHED SIZE

About 19 (21, 23)" (48.5 [53.5, 58.5] cm) head circumference measured just above the ears, and 43½ (48¼, 53¼)" (110.5 [122.5, 135.5] cm) outer brim circumference. Hat shown measures 21" (53.5 cm) head circumference.

YARN

Sportweight (CYCA #2 Fine) for MC; worsted weight (CYCA #4 Medium) for CC.

Shown here: GGH Merino Soft (100% merino; 186 yd [170 m]/50 g): #15 black (MC), 2 balls.

Muench Touch Me (72% microfiber, 28% wool; 61 yd [56 m]/50 g): #3826 chocolate brown (CC), 2 balls.

NEEDLES

Size 4 (3.5 mm): 16" and 24" (40 and 60 cm) circular (cir) and set of 4 or 5 double-pointed (dpn). Size 6 (4 mm): 32" (80 cm) cir. Adjust needle size if necessary to obtain the correct gauge.

NOTIONS

Markers (m; 1 in a contrasting color for end of rnd); tapestry needle; pillowcase, dishtowels, and bowl for making hatblock; size G/6 (4.25 mm) crochet hook; size E/4 (3.5 mm) or D/3 (3.25 mm) crochet hook; heavy-weight sewing thread such as buttonhole twist; about 9 yd (8.25 m) of black 18-gauge millinery wire; pliers with wire cutters.

GAUGE

27 sts and 34 rows = 4" (10 cm) in stockinette stitch with MC using smaller needles (see Notes for how to work gauge swatch).

Trinity Lace: (multiple of 6 sts plus 3)

Row 1: (RS) *Yo, sl 2 sts as if to k2tog, k1, pass 2 slipped sts over (p2sso), yo, k3; rep from * to last 3 sts, yo, sl 2 as if to k2tog, k1, p2sso, yo.

Rows 2 and 4: (WS) Purl.

Row 3: *K3, yo, sl 2 sts as if to k2tog, k1, p2sso, yo; rep from * to last 3 sts, k3.

Repeat Rows 1–4 for pattern.

BRIM

With MC and shorter smaller-size cir needle, CO 117 (130, 143) sts. Do not join for working in the rnd. Knit 2 rows—1 garter st ridge. *Next row:* (RS) Place marker (pm) of contrasting color, *k13, place 2 markers next to each other; rep from * 7 (8, 9) more times, k13. Join for working in the rnd, being careful not to twist sts. *Next rnd:* *Work first 13 sts according to Rnd 1 of Brim chart, slip marker (sl m), yo, sl m; rep from * 8 (9, 10) more times—126 (140, 154) sts. Cont in patt until Rnd 32 has been completed, inc as shown on chart and changing to longer smaller-size cir needle when there are too many sts to fit comfortably around the shorter cir needle—261 (290, 319) sts.

Brim Edging

Change to CC and larger cir needle.

Rnd 1: *[K2tog twice, k1] 5 times, k2tog twice; rep from * 8 (9, 10) more times—153 (170, 187) sts.

Rnd 2: *K2, yo, k3, yo, k7, yo, k5; rep from * 8 (9, 10) more times—180 (200, 220) sts.

Rnds 3 and 5: Knit.

Rnd 4: *K2, yo, k5, yo, k8, M1 (see Glossary, page 155), k5; rep from * 8 (9, 10) more times—207 (230, 253) sts.

Rnd 6: *K2, yo, k7, yo, k8, yo, k6; rep from * 8 (9, 10) more times—234 (260, 286) sts.

Rnd 7: Knit, removing markers between reps as you come to them.

With knitting needle or larger crochet hook as desired, BO all sts using the picot method (see Stitch Guide).

CROWN

With MC, shorter smaller-size cir needle, and RS facing, pick up and knit 1 st from each CO st along inner edge of brim, pm every 13 sts, and using a contrasting m at end of rnd—117 (130, 143) sts. Work Rnds 1–19 of Crown chart, changing to dpn when there are too few sts to fit around cir needle—9 (10, 11) sts rem. Cut yarn, leaving an 8" (20.5 cm) tail. Thread tail on tapestry needle, draw through rem sts, pull tight to close top of crown, and fasten off to WS. Weave in loose ends.

Legend

- ☐ knit
- • purl
- ╱ k2tog
- ╲ ssk
- ○ yo
- Ⓜ M1 (see Glossary, page 155)
- ⋀ sl 2 sts as if to k2tog, k1, p2sso
- ⓢ sl 3 sts as if to k3tog, ssk, p3sso
- ▮ marker position

Crown

(chart rows, right side numbered odd: 1, 3, 5, 7, 9, 11, 13, 15, 17, 19)

Brim

(chart rows, right side numbered odd: 1, 3, 5, 7, 9, 11, 13, 15, 17, 19, 21, 23, 25, 27, 29, 31)

HATBAND

With CC and larger cir needle, CO 43 sts. Do not join for working in the rnd. Knit 3 rows. Establish Trinity Lace patt (see Stitch Guide) on next row as foll: (RS) K2 (edge sts; work in garter st), work Row 1 of Trinity Lace patt across center 39 sts, k2 (edge sts; work in garter st). Knitting the first 2 and last 2 sts of every row for edge sts, cont in Trinity Lace patt until piece measures 6" (15 cm) from CO, ending with a WS row. *Next row:* (RS) K2, *k3tog; rep from * to last 2 sts, k2—17 sts rem. Work even in garter st until garter section is long enough to wrap easily around the base of the crown, ending with a WS row. *Next row:* (RS) K2, *knit into back of next st but do not sl from needle, yo, knit into front of same st, sl st from needle (3 sts made from 1 st); rep from * to last 2 sts, k2—43 sts. Change to Trinity Lace and beg with Row 2, work in lace patt for 6" (15 cm), ending with a RS row. Knit 3 rows. BO all sts loosely.

FINISHING

Roll three to four dishtowels into a ball that is roughly the size of your head. Place ball in a pillowcase and pull the case snugly around it. With a piece of yarn, tie the pillowcase closed, holding the towel ball tightly in place. Set this pillowcase hatblock in a small bowl, letting the excess pillowcase lie inside the bowl. Set the bowl on top of an upside-down bowl or box to add more height if the block seems too low.

Blocking

The shape of the hat is achieved by blocking, wiring, and placement of the hatband. Survey the hat and determine which side you'd like for the front. Mark the inside back with a loop of waste yarn. Wet the crown of the hat (try not to get the brim too wet) by holding it under warm running water. *Gently* squeeze out excess water from crown, but *do not twist or wring.* Place wet crown firmly over hatblock, pulling bottom edge of brim evenly. Use your hands to smooth the crown (you shouldn't need to pin the crown in place). Allow hat to air-dry *thoroughly.*

Just about everything looks better in lace.

Headsize Wire

Measure the wearer's head circumference or use the Finished Size information for this project as a guide. Cut a length of millinery wire 1½" (3.8 cm) longer than head circumference. Cut an 18" (45.5 cm) length of heavy thread and make a slipknot at one end. Tighten slipknot around one end of wire. Overlap ends of wire 1" (2.5 cm) and wrap heavy thread tightly around the overlapped area, paying special attention to the cut ends of the wire and being careful not to create a large bump by using too much thread in any one area. Finish off the thread by knotting it around the wire, then weaving it back under the wrapped strands. Turn hat inside out. There will be a noticeable ridge where the crown sts were picked up along the CO edge of brim; this is called the headsize. With MC and smaller crochet hook, attach headsize wire along the headsize as foll: Rest the headsize wire circle on top of the headsize edge and gently hold both tog in your left hand. Working beneath the wire, push crochet hook through next st along the headsize edge and pull up a loop. *Cont working beneath the headsize wire, pull a loop of yarn back through the next st—2 loops on hook. Working above the wire,

pull the yarn through both loops on hook to enclose the wire. Rep from * around. Fasten off. Weave in loose ends.

Prepare Brim Wire

With WS facing, very lightly steam-block the hat brim. "Spring" or straighten the brim wire by running it slowly between your thumb and index finger, keeping pressure against the natural curve of the wire, until you have sprung a length a bit more than twice the distance around the outer edge of the brim, using the Finished Size information for this project as a guide. When springing the wire, move your thumb *slowly* over the wire; if you move too fast, you can get a wire burn. Cut an 18" (45.5 cm) length of heavy thread and make a slipknot at the end. Place slipknot over one end of the wire and tighten. Lay the sprung wire around the outer edge of the brim so that the circumference of the wire is about 1" (2.5 cm) larger than the hat brim. Without cutting the wire, temporarily tape the wire circle closed at this point. Begin doubling the brim wire by working more wire around the established circumference and wrapping both thicknesses of wire together with the thread—wraps should be about ⅛" (3 mm) apart and should be rather tight. Cont working around the brim wire, adding to the thread as necessary by tying on additional 18" (45.5 cm) lengths (the knots will be covered when the hat is attached to the brim). Work until the entire brim wire is doubled, then work 1" (2.5 cm) beyond the taped area (removing the tape as you work past that part). Cut the wire. Wrap the thread very tightly around the doubled ends of the wire, making sure to cover the cut ends as thoroughly as possible without creating a bulky bump. Finish off the thread by knotting it around the wire, then weaving it back under the wrapped strands. Working back around the brim, weave all loose ends into the wrapped strands in the same manner.

Attach Brim Wire

With CC and larger crochet hook, attach brim wire to outer BO edge of hat brim as foll: Hold hat brim right side up in your left hand. Insert crochet hook into a st along the outer edge of the brim and draw up a loop on the hook. Rest the brim wire circle on top of the brim and gently hold both tog in your left hand. *Working beneath the wire, push crochet hook through next st along the outer edge and pull up a loop—2 loops on hook. Working above the wire, pull the yarn through both loops on hook to enclose the wire. Rep from * around, stretching the brim to fit tautly and evenly to the wire circle. *Note:* In order to completely cover the wire, and depending on the thickness of the yarn, it may be necessary to work more than 1 crochet st into each knitted st along outer edge. Fasten off. Weave in loose ends.

Attach Hatband

Arrange hatband loosely around base of crown with Trinity Lace ends overlapping as shown in photograph to create a faux bow effect. Sew hatband to hat using CC threaded on a tapestry needle.

Whether you wear it up over your head or down around your neck, a wimple—especially one that's edged in lace—makes a delicate frame for your face. In this version, **Priscilla Gibson-Roberts** worked a decorative edging pattern back and forth in rows and joined it into a ring for the lower border. She then picked up stitches around the straight edge of the border and worked circularly to the top in stockinette stitch, finishing off with a simple eyelet pattern bordered by a few garter ridges.

LOWER EDGING

Note: Lower edging is worked back and forth in rows. With waste yarn and using the provisional method (see Glossary, page 152), CO 15 sts.

Row 1: (RS) K9, [yo, k2tog] 2 times, yo, k2—16 sts.

Row 2: (WS) Use the backward loop method (see Glossary, page 152) to CO 2 sts, BO the 2 sts just CO to form a short "fringe," knit to end.

Row 3: K10, [yo, k2tog] 2 times, yo, k2—17 sts.

Row 4: CO 3 sts as before, BO these 3 sts, knit to end.

Row 5: K11, [yo, k2tog] 2 times, yo, k2—18 sts.

Row 6: CO 4 sts as before, BO these 4 sts, knit to end.

Row 7: K12, [yo, k2tog] 2 times, yo, k2—19 sts.

Row 8: CO 5 sts as before, BO these 5 sts, knit to end.

Row 9: K13, [yo, k2tog] 2 times, yo, k2—20 sts.

Row 10: CO 6 sts as before, BO these 6 sts, knit to end.

Row 11: K11, [k2tog, yo] 3 times, k2tog, k1—19 sts rem.

Row 12: Rep Row 8.

Row 13: K10, [k2tog, yo] 3 times, k2tog, k1—18 sts rem.

Row 14: Rep Row 6.

Row 15: K9, [k2tog, yo] 3 times, k2tog, k1—17 sts rem.

Row 16: Rep Row 4.

Row 17: K8, [k2tog, yo] 3 times, k2tog, k1—16 sts rem.

Row 18: Rep Row 2.

Row 19: K7, [k2tog, yo] 3 times, k2tog, k1—15 sts rem.

FINISHED SIZE

About 20" (51 cm) circumference at upper edge and 13½" (34.5 cm) total length measured at deepest point of lower edging.

YARN

Laceweight (no CYCA equivalent).

Shown here: KnitPicks Shadow (100% merino wool; 440 yd [402 m]/50 g): #23661 sunset, 2 skeins.

NEEDLES

Size 2 (2.5 mm): 16" (40 cm) circular. Adjust needle size if necessary to obtain the correct gauge.

NOTIONS

Smooth waste yarn for invisible cast-on; stitch marker (m); tapestry needle.

GAUGE

36 stitches and 44 rounds = 4" (10 cm) in stockinette stitch worked in the round.

Row 20: K15.

Rep these 20 rows 23 more times—24 patt reps total; 480 rows total; piece measures about 30" (76 cm) from CO. Carefully remove waste yarn from invisible CO and place 15 live sts on needle. Holding ends of edging with RS facing tog, use the three-needle method (see Glossary, page 151) to bind off the CO and BO ends tog to form a ring.

CENTER SECTION

With RS of edging facing, beg at seam, and working along the straight edge of the ring, pick up and knit 1 st from the "valley" between the each garter ridge—240 sts. Place marker (pm), and join for working in the rnd.

Rnd 1: Purl.

Rnd 2: *K14, k2tog; rep from *—225 sts rem.

Rnds 3 and 5: Purl.

Rnd 4: *K13, k2tog; rep from *—210 sts rem.

Rnd 6: *K12, k2tog; rep from *—195 sts rem.

Rnds 7–18: Knit.

Rnd 19: *K11, k2tog; rep from *—180 sts rem.

Cont even in St st (knit every rnd) until St st section measures 9¼" (23.5 cm) above last garter ridge (Rnd 5), or until piece measures about 12¼" (31 cm) from deepest point of lower edging.

TOP EDGING

Rnd 1: Purl.

Rnd 2: Knit.

Rnds 3–6: Rep Rnds 1 and 2 two more times.

Rnds 7 and 8: Knit.

Rnds 9 and 11: *K7, k2tog, yo, k3; rep from *.

Rnds 10 and 12: *K6, k2tog, yo, k1, yo, k2tog, k1; rep from *.

Rnds 13 and 14: Knit.

Rnds 15–20: Rep Rnds 1–6.

BO all sts loosely.

FINISHING

Weave in loose ends. Lightly steam-block to open up the lower and top edgings; the wider bottom end of the wimple will flare out at the base.

Sometimes just
a little bit of
lace is just right.

Annie Modesitt has used fine silver wire to knit this classy little bracelet on large needles that exaggerate the open stitches of a simple pattern. Unlike normal knitting yarns, the wire stretches to fit over the hand, then can be reshaped to fit the wrist. Swarovski glass crystals give a ruffled look to the cast-on and bind-off edges. The cuff is knitted circularly in just twelve simple rounds—you'll be done before you know it!

NOTES
❖ To put on the bracelet, insert your index fingers into the bracelet cylinder, one from each end. Using a hand-over-hand rolling motion, tug gently to widen the circumference until the bracelet is just large enough to fit over your hand. Once the bracelet is on your wrist, trap the upper edge of the bracelet against the base of your palm using the fingertips of your bracelet hand, and use your other hand to tug gently all the way around the lower edge of the bracelet to stretch it long and narrow to fit your wrist.

FINISHED SIZE
About 8" (20.5 cm) circumference and 3" (7.5 cm) wide.

YARN
26-gauge wire.
Shown here: Habu AC-1 Fine Silver 30-Gauge Wire (50 yd [45 m]/spool): silver, 1 spool.

NEEDLES
Size 5 (3.75 mm): set of 4 double-pointed (dpn). *Note:* Aluminum needles are best for working with wire.

NOTIONS
28 Swarovski crystal 6 mm cube beads; marker (m); needle-nose pliers; strong scissors or wire cutter; clear nail polish (optional).

GAUGE
Exact gauge is not critical for this project.

Knitted lace doesn't have to be knitted with yarn.

PREPARATION
String all beads onto the wire.

BRACELET
Using the long-tail method (see Glossary, page 153), CO 42 sts as foll: *CO 3 sts, slip bead next to needle; rep from * 13 more times—42 sts and 14 beads on needle. Divide sts evenly on 3 dpn (14 sts each needle), place marker (pm), and join for working in the rnd, being careful not to twist sts. Knit 1 rnd.

Rnd 1: *K1, yo, k3tog, yo, k2; rep from * to end of rnd.

Rnd 2: Knit.

Rep Rnds 1 and 2 five more times—12 rnds of patt total; piece measures about 3" (7.5 cm) from CO; exact measurement is not critical. *Next rnd:* Sl each st individually kwise so that the trailing leg of each st is in front of the needle (this will make the BO easier; do *not* actually knit any sts in this rnd). BO all sts as foll: *[K2tog through back loops (tbl), sl st just created back onto left-hand needle] 3 times, slip bead next to needle; rep from * 13 more times—all sts bound off; bead placed after every 3rd st.

Delicate wire and faceted crystal beads add sparkle to a knitted bracelet.

FINISHING

Pull each loose wire end through the bracelet at the CO or BO edge to create a loop and a tail resembling the number 6. Use pliers to twist the loop and the single tail tog to create a 3-strand twist about ⅝" (1.5 cm) long. With strong scissors or wire cutters, trim the piece to ½" (1.3 cm). With pliers, coil this twisted strand and crimp it (press it very tightly) against the inside of the piece. As you press the spiral in the pliers, be careful not to inadvertently squeeze and break any beads. *Tip:* After coiling the twisted loose ends of wire and crimping in place, you can add a dot of clear nail polish to the crimped area to conceal the sharp ends.

SHETLAND SHAWL TURNED VEST
VÉRONIK AVERY

Véronik Avery took inspiration from the classic Shetland shawl for this little charcoal vest. She combined two lace patterns: one typically used to create the shawl's outer edge for the lower part of her vest, and one typically used in the shawl's interior area for the bodice. The crossover straps have picot details that continue around the neck and armholes. Narrow silver and teal stripes set off the lower body edge and line the straps. The soft wool yarn that Véronik used forms gentle halos around the lace patterns.

> **NOTE**
> ❖ When shaping the front armholes and neck in the openwork rib pattern, if there are not enough stitches to work both yarnovers and the double decrease between them in Row 1 of the pattern, work the available stitches in stockinette instead to avoid throwing off the stitch count.

STITCH GUIDE

Moss Stitch: (worked over 3 sts)
Row 1: (RS) K1, p1, k1.
Row 2 and 3: P1, k1, p1.
Row 4: K1, p1, k1.
Repeat Rows 1–4 for pattern.

Openwork Rib: (multiple of 5 sts + 2)
Row 1: (RS) K1, *p1, yo, sl 1, k2tog, psso, yo, p1; rep from * to last st, k1.
Rows 2 and 4: (WS) P1, *k1, p3, k1; rep from * to last st, p1.
Row 3: K1, *p1, k3, p1; rep from * to last st, k1.
Repeat Rows 1–4 for pattern.

FINISHED SIZE
31¼ (35¼, 39¾, 45¼)" (79.5 [89.5, 101, 115] cm) bust/chest circumference. Vest shown measures 31¼" (79.5 cm).

YARN
Sportweight (CYCA #2 Fine).
Shown here: Reynolds Whiskey (100% wool; 195 yd [178 m]/50 g): #59 charcoal, 4 (6, 7, 8) balls; #53 teal and #31 silver, 1 ball each.

NEEDLES
Body—size 3 (3.25 mm): straight. Edging—size 2 (3 mm): 32" (80 cm) or longer circular (cir). Adjust needle size if necessary to obtain the correct gauge.

NOTIONS
Markers (m); cable needle (cn); stitch holders; tapestry needle; two ¾" (2 cm) buttons (optional).

GAUGE
34 stitches = 5¼" (13.5 cm) and 14 rows = 1¼" (3.2 cm) of Arrow Lace chart using larger needles; 14 stitches = 2⅛" (5.4 cm) and 36 rows = 3¾" (9.5 cm) in Rows 1–6 of Totem Lace chart using larger needles; 21½ stitches and 40½ rows = 4" (10 cm) in openwork rib pattern using larger needles.

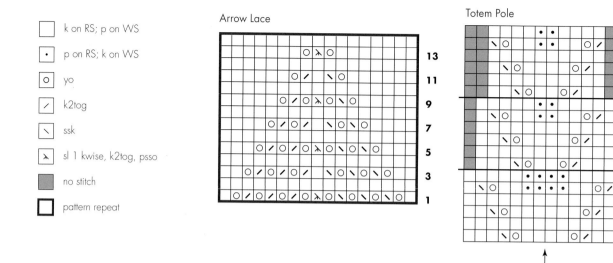

☐	k on RS; p on WS
•	p on RS; k on WS
○	yo
∕	k2tog
＼	ssk
λ	sl 1 kwise, k2tog, psso
▨	no stitch
☐	pattern repeat

Arrow Lace

Totem Pole

center

*Dec the first time this row is worked as given in directions.

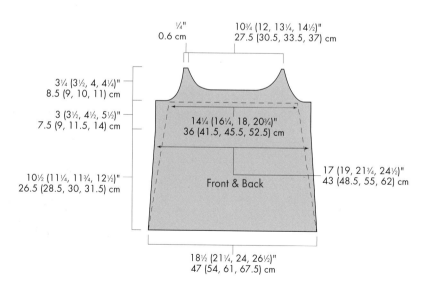

¼"
0.6 cm

10¾ (12, 13¼, 14½)"
27.5 (30.5, 33.5, 37) cm

3¼ (3½, 4, 4¼)"
8.5 (9, 10, 11) cm

3 (3½, 4½, 5½)"
7.5 (9, 11.5, 14) cm

14¼ (16¼, 18, 20¾)"
36 (41.5, 45.5, 52.5) cm

17 (19, 21¾, 24½)"
43 (48.5, 55, 62) cm

Front & Back

10½ (11¼, 11¾, 12½)"
26.5 (28.5, 30, 31.5) cm

18½ (21¼, 24, 26½)"
47 (54, 61, 67.5) cm

BACK

With silver and smaller needle, CO 121 (138, 155, 172) sts. Knit 1 WS row. Change to larger needles. *Set-up row:* (RS) K1 (selvedge st), work Row 1 of Arrow Lace chart across center 119 (136, 153, 170) sts, k1 (selvedge st). Maintaining selvedge sts in St st throughout, work Row 2 of chart with silver, Rows 3–6 with teal, and Rows 7–14 with charcoal. Cont to end of back with charcoal and establish patt from Row 1 of moss st (see Stitch Guide) and Totem Pole chart as foll: (RS) K1 (selvedge st), work 7 sts from center to end of Totem Pole chart once, [work 3 sts in moss st, work 14 sts of Totem Pole chart] 6 (7, 8, 9) times, work 3 sts in moss st, work 7 sts from beg of Totem Pole chart to center once, k1 (selvedge st). Maintaining selvedge sts and moss st as established, rep Rows 1–6 *only* of Totem Pole chart a total of 6 (7, 8, 9) times—36 (42, 48, 54) rows total of Totem Pole chart; piece measures about 5 (5½, 6¼, 6¾)" (12.5 [14, 16, 17] cm) from CO. *Dec row:* (RS; counts as Row 7 of chart) K1 (selvedge st), k1, yo, ssk, k2, k2tog, [work 3 sts in moss st, ssk, k2, k2tog, yo, k2, yo, ssk, k2, k2tog] 6 (7, 8, 9) times, work 3 sts in moss st, ssk, k2, k2tog, yo, k1, k1 (selvedge st)—107 (122, 137, 152) sts rem; each full Totem Pole patt has been dec'd to 12 sts, and each half patt at end of row has been dec'd to 6 sts. Maintaining selvedge sts, cont in patt as established, working Rows 8–12 of Totem Pole chart once, then rep Rows 7–12 *only* 3 times—piece measures about 7½ (8¼, 8¾, 9½)" (19 [21, 22, 24] cm) from CO. *Dec row:* (RS; counts as Row 13 of chart) K1 (selvedge st), k1, yo, ssk, k1, k2tog, [work 3 sts in moss st, ssk, k1, k2tog, yo, k2, yo, ssk, k1, k2tog] 6 (7, 8, 9) times, work 3 sts in moss st, ssk, k1, k2tog, yo, k1, k1 (selvedge st)—93 (106, 119, 132) sts rem; each full Totem Pole patt has been dec'd to 10 sts, and each half patt at end of row has been dec'd to 5 sts. Maintaining selvedge sts, cont in patt as established, working Rows 14–18 of Totem Pole chart once, then rep Rows 13–18 *only* 4 times—piece measures about 10½ (11¼, 11¾, 12½)" (26.5 [28.5, 30, 31.5] cm) from CO. *Dec row:* (RS) K1, [k5, sl 1, k2tog, psso, k5] 7 (8, 9, 10) times, k1—79 (90, 101, 112) sts rem. Knit 1 WS row for garter ridge, dec 2 (3, 4, 0) sts evenly spaced—77 (87, 97, 112) sts

rem. Change to openwork rib patt (see Stitch Guide), and work in patt until piece measures 3 (3½, 4½, 5½)" (7.5 [9, 11.5, 14] cm) above garter ridge. Place all sts on holder.

FRONT

CO and work as for back until Totem Pole chart has been completed—93 (106, 119, 132) sts; piece measures about 10½ (11¼, 11¾, 12½)" (26.5 [28.5, 30, 31.5] cm) from CO. Knit 2 rows for garter ridge, dec 1 (4, 2, 0) st(s) evenly on last row—92 (102, 117, 132) sts rem. Change to openwork rib patt, and work in patt until piece measures 3 (3½, 4½, 5½)" (7.5 [9, 11.5, 14] cm) from garter ridge.

Shape Armholes

Cont in openwork rib patt (see Note), BO 5 (5, 7, 9) sts at beg of next 2 rows, then BO 2 sts at beg of foll 10 (12, 14, 16) rows—62 (68, 75, 82) sts rem.

Shape Neck

Cont in openwork rib patt, work 20 (22, 24, 26) sts, join a new ball of yarn and BO center 22 (24, 27, 30) sts, work to end—20 (22, 24, 26) sts each side. Working each side separately, at each neck edge BO 2 sts 9 (10, 11, 12) times—2 sts rem each side; armholes measure about 3¼ (3½, 4, 4¼)" (8.5 [9, 10, 11] cm). Cut yarn, thread tail through rem sts, and pull tight to fasten off.

FINISHING

Straps and Front Edging

With charcoal, smaller needle, and using the knitted method (see Glossary, page 152), CO 98 (100, 102, 104) sts for left strap, then with same needle, pick up and knit 62 (68, 75, 82) sts across front neck, then onto the same needle, CO 98 (100, 102, 104) sts for right strap—258 (268, 279, 290) sts total. Knit 1 WS row for garter ridge. Work 4 rows even in St st, ending with a WS row. *Picot row:* (RS) *K2tog, yo; rep from * to last 2 (2, 1, 2) st(s), k2 (2, 1, 2). Change to silver and work 2 rows in St st. Change to teal and work 2 more rows in St st. BO all sts.

Straps and Side/Back Edging

With yarn threaded on a tapestry needle, sew side seams. With charcoal and smaller cir needle, pick up and knit 97 (99, 101, 103) sts along CO row of right strap, 26 (29, 35, 41) sts along right armhole, k77 (87, 97, 112) back sts from holder, pick up and knit 26 (29, 35, 41) sts along left armhole, and 97 (99, 101, 103) sts along CO row of left strap—323 (343, 369, 400) sts total. Knit 1 WS row for garter ridge. Work 4 rows even in St st, ending with a WS row. *Picot row:* (RS) *K2tog, yo; rep from * to last 1 (1, 1, 2) st(s), k1 (1, 1, 2). Change to silver and work 2 rows St st. Change to teal and work 2 more rows in St st. BO all sts.

Fold edgings to WS along center picot rows. With yarn threaded on a tapestry needle, stitch edgings to WS of front neck and top edge of back. Bring BO rows tog at center on underside of each strap, and sew BO edges tog. Weave in loose ends. Try vest on and mark position of straps on back, adjusting placement for best fit. Secure ends of straps to back, sewing a button on top of each end, if desired. For the vest shown, the straps were crossed in back and attached 4" (10 cm) apart in the center of the upper back.

Take inspiration from traditional lace patterns and applications.

designNOTEBOOK

RETRO REDUX SHRUG
mercedes tarasovich-clark

THE ESSENTIAL TANK
laura zukaite

ANY TYPE OF LACE IS FORMED BY the simple interplay of open holes against a solid background. In knitting, the holes are formed by yarnover increases worked on a background of stockinette or garter stitch fabric. To emphasize the holes and to maintain a consistent stitch count, the yarnover increases are worked in conjunction with decreases. The type of decrease used and its placement in relationship to the yarnover result in defining lines that help emphasize the openwork pattern. It is the interplay between holes, lines, and solid backgrounds that characterize knitted lace.

To create an airy fabric, lace is generally worked with fine yarn on needles larger than would be used for stockinette stitch in the same yarn. After knitting, the fabric is stretched and blocked to reveal the openwork pattern.

Knitted lace motifs can be used as allover patterns, as in Shirley Paden's Ooh La Lace Dress and Stole (page 64) and Laura Zukaite's The Essential Tank (page 50); as panels or inserts, as in Kathy Zimmerman's Katharine Hepburn Cardigan (page 78) and Norah Gaughan's Lacy Waves Top (page 104); or as edgings, such as in Nancy Bush's Lily of the Valley Shawl (page 20) and Mari Lynn Patrick's Just Right Wrap (page 12). However it is used, the interplay of holes, lines, and solid areas produces an array of beautiful knitted lace designs.

Some lace aficionados make a distinction between the two types of lace produced by knitting: *knitted lace*, in which the increases and decreases are worked on both right- and wrong-side rows, and *lace knitting*, in which the increases and decreases are worked on right-side rows only. For the purposes of this book the two terms are used interchangeably.

WAYS TO KNIT LACE

To make lace, you simply need to know how to make yarnovers and decreases and how to count the stitches in between the two. But before you can begin to design with lace, you need to understand the structures of these yarnovers and decreases.

YARNOVER INCREASES

Yarnovers are made in slightly different ways depending on what kind of stitches—knit or purl—precede or follow them. When working right-side rows of stockinette or garter stitch, a yarnover is made between two knit stitches. Simply wrap the yarn around the needle from front to back (Figure 1). To work a yarnover after a knit stitch and before a purl stitch, bring the yarn to the front under the needle, around the top of the needle to the back, then under the needle again to the front (Figure 2). Between two purl stitches, work the yarnover by bringing the yarn over the top of the needle (front to back), then around the bottom of the needle to the front again (Figure 3). Work a yarnover after a purl stitch and before a knit stitch by bringing the yarn over the top of the needle from front to back (Figure 4).

Figure 1. Yarnover between two knit stitches.

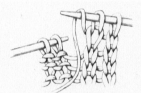

Figure 2. Yarnover after a knit stitch and before a purl stitch.

Figure 3. Yarnover between two purl stitches.

Figure 4. Yarnover after a purl stitch and before a knit stitch.

LILY OF THE VALLEY SHAWL

nancy bush

KATHARINE HEPBURN CARDIGAN

kathy zimmerman

JUST RIGHT WRAP
mari lynn patrick

All you need to know is how to make yarnovers and decreases and how to count stitches.

DECREASES

The way stitches are worked together to make a decrease causes the resulting stitch to slant to the left or to the right, or to remain vertically aligned. This distinction, although subtle between individual stitches, is important because it's fundamental to creating the prominent, "defining" lines in lace patterns. (All of the examples shown here are for stitches mounted on the needle in the conventional manner—leading leg in front—when knitting off the left needle onto the right needle.)

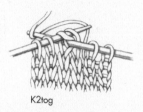

K2tog

Right Slant

Knit 2 Together (k2tog)
The simplest decrease, k2tog, is made by knitting two stitches together as if they were a single stitch. The second stitch (the one on the left) lies on top of the first, causing the decrease to slant to the right.

Left Slant

Slip 1, Knit 1, Pass Slipped Stitch Over (sl 1, k1, psso)
A near mirror image of the k2tog decrease, the sl 1, k1, psso decrease is made so that the first stitch (the one on the right) lies on top of the second, causing the decrease to slant to the left. To work this type of decrease, slip one stitch knitwise, knit the next stitch (Figure 1), then use the left needle tip to lift the slipped stitch up and over the knitted stitch (Figure 2) and off the right needle.

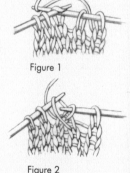

Figure 1

Figure 2

Slip, Slip, Knit (ssk)
The ssk decrease looks much the same as sl 1, k1, psso, but it is done in fewer movements, and is favored by many knitters. To make this left-leaning decrease, slip two stitches individually knitwise (Figure 1), insert the left needle through the front of the two slipped stitches, and knit them together through their back loops (Figure 2).

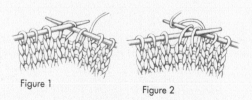

Figure 1

Figure 2

Double Decreases

Sometimes you'll want to decrease two stitches at the same time. Again, the way the decrease is made will result in a stitch that slants to the right, to the left, or doesn't slant at all.

Right Slant

To make a right-slanting double decrease, slip one stitch knitwise to the right needle, knit one stitch, pass the slipped stitch over the knitted stitch (Figure 1), return the decreased stitch to the left needle, then pass the second stitch

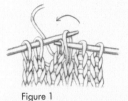

Figure 1

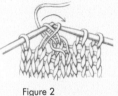

Figure 2

on the left needle over the decreased stitch (Figure 2) and return the decreased stitch to the right needle.

An alternate method that is much simpler to execute is to knit three stitches together (k3tog).

Left Slant

For a left-slanting decrease, slip one stitch knitwise to the right needle, knit the next two stitches together (Figure 1), then use the tip of the left needle to lift the slipped stitch up and over the knitted stitches (Figure 2) and off the needle.

Figure 1

An alternate method that has a more pronounced left slant is a modification of the ssk decrease, abbreviated sssk: slip three stitches individually knitwise, then knit them together through their back loops.

Figure 2

Centered

For a double decrease that is vertically aligned, slip two stitches together knitwise to the right needle (Figure 1), knit the next stitch (Figure 2), then use the tip of the left needle to lift the two slipped stitches up and over the knitted stitch (Figure 3) and off the needle.

Figure 1

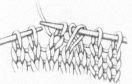

Figure 2

Figure 3

PEEK-A-BOO CLOCHE
mona schmidt

Double decreases can slant to the right, the left, or they can be vertically aligned.

Swatch 1

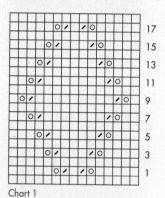

Chart 1

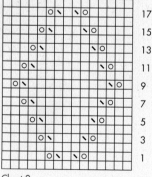

Swatch 2

Chart 2

See page 141 for chart symbol key.

THE INTERPLAY OF YARNOVERS AND DECREASES

Yarnovers and decreases can be combined to form many lacy effects—the decrease may slant to the right or left; it may be right next to the yarnover or several stitches away; or even on a completely different row. Such differences can have a marked effect on the appearance of the openwork pattern.

YARNOVERS NEXT TO DECREASES

Right-Leaning Decreases

In Swatch 1 and Chart 1, all of the decreases slant to the right (k2tog). In the lower half of the sample diamond motif, the yarnovers are worked before the decreases for the lower right side and after the decreases for the lower left side. The yarnovers are barely visible on the lower right because as the yarnovers travel to the right on subsequent rows, they are immediately used up in the decreases, effectively closing up the holes. The holes on the lower left are more visible because the decreases are worked before the yarnovers, but the eyelets are also small because the decreases involve the stitches formed by the yarnovers from previous rows, again closing the holes.

On the top half of the diamond, the eyelets are noticeably larger, because none of the decreases in this section interact with the yarnovers in the immediately previous rows. On the upper right side, the yarnovers are worked before the decreases, and the decreases, which travel to the left, help to enlarge the eyelet. The definition of each eyelet along the upper left side is further enhanced because the right-slanting decreases pull the adjacent stitches away from the yarnovers. Moreover, the decreases align with each other to form a distinct defining line that borders and enhances the eyelets.

Left-Leaning Decreases

The only difference between Swatch 2 (Chart 2) and the previous swatch is that all the decreases are left-leaning ssk, instead of right-leaning k2tog decreases. There's not much difference in the appearance of the lower half of the diamond—again, all of the decreases in this area are placed on top of the yarnovers of the previous pattern row, thereby closing up the eyelets. But the top half of the diamond is a mirror image of the top half of Swatch 1. All of the eyelets are larger because, instead of working to close up the holes, the decreases help to pull them open. On the upper right side, the decreased stitches align with each other to form a distinct line that enhances the eyelets.

Lace designers use these characteristics to their advantage when designing lace patterns. The general objective of knitted lace is visible eyelets. The sample in Swatch 3 (Chart 3) combines

Swatch 3

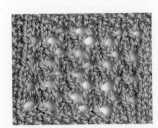

Swatch 4

Swatch 5

Swatch 6

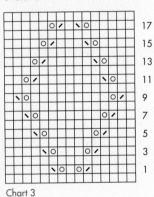

Chart 3

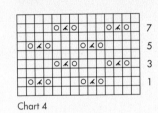

Chart 4

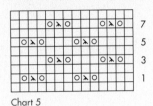

Chart 5

Chart 6

the parts of Swatch 1 and Swatch 2 that maximize the size of the eyelets and the prominence of defining lines. This is the most common arrangement in lace designs—right-leaning decreases before eyelets that travel to the right and left-leaning decreases after eyelets that travel to the left.

DOUBLE DECREASES

Some patterns call for two yarnovers separated by a double decrease, as in Pam Allen's Little Silk Shrug (page 46). Just like single decreases, double decreases can be made to slant to the left or right. They can also be made with no slant at all. Again, the differences are subtle. Right-leaning double decreases are used in Swatch 4 (Chart 4), left-leaning decreases are used in Swatch 5 (Chart 5), and centered decreases are used in Swatch 6 (Chart 6).

YARNOVERS AND DECREASES SEPARATED A FEW STITCHES

Many lace patterns have several stitches separating the yarnovers and their companion decreases, as in Annie Modesitt's Greta Garbo Garden Hat (page 110). No matter which type of decrease is used, the separating stitches will slant toward the decrease of the yarnover/decrease pair, giving the separating stitches a biased effect. The biased stitches are best defined when left-leaning decreases are combined with stitches that bias to the left and right-leaning decreases are combined with stitches that bias to the right, as in Swatch 7 (Chart 7).

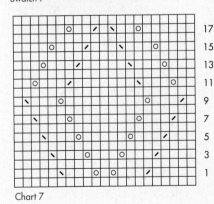

Swatch 7

Chart 7

See page 141 for chart symbol key.

Swatch 8

Chart 8

Swatch 10

Chart 10

Swatch 9

Chart 9

See page 141 for chart symbol key.

UNEVEN EDGES

All of the swatches previously mentioned have yarnovers offset or staggered from row to row. However, some patterns call for the yarnovers and decreases to be stacked one on top of another. If the decrease is always worked on the same side of the yarnover, the cast-on and bind-off edges will slant in the direction of the decrease—if the decrease is to the left of the yarnover, the edge will slant downward toward the left; if the decrease is to the right of the yarnover, the fabric will slant downward to the right. On the right half of Swatch 8 (Chart 8), the decreases are consistently made after the yarnovers; on the left half they are made before the yarnovers. Notice how the overall shape of the swatch forms a V; the right half slants down to the left, the left half slants down to the right. The effect is the same whether right- or left-slant decreases are used. Véronik Avery used this idea to create small scallops at the lower edge (i.e., the cast-on edge) of her Shetland Shawl Turned Vest (page 124). To maintain straight cast-on and bind-off edges, as in the hem trim on Michele Rose Orne's Lace-Edged Corset (page 30), the decreases are placed on alternate sides of the yarnovers, as in Swatch 9 (Chart 9). The selvedge edges will slant if all of the decreases are on the same side of the yarnovers, as in Swatch 10 (Chart 10). You can make the selvedges zig and zag if the decreases are

Swatch 11

Swatch 12

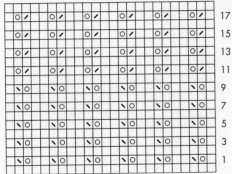
Chart 11

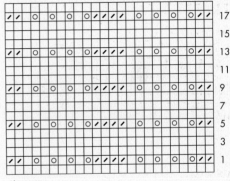
Chart 12

consistently worked on one side of the yarnovers on one row or set of rows, then on the other side of the yarnovers on the following row or set of rows, as in Swatch 11 (Chart 11). Lisa Daehlin used this principle to make the zigzag lace panels in her Leg Cozies (page 100), but because she worked the leggings in the round, there are no selvedge edges.

You can get different effects by grouping the yarnovers and decreases. Swatch 12 (Chart 12), a classic pattern called Feather and Fan, calls for alternating groups of yarnovers with groups of decreases, all on the same row. The number of stitches is constant from row to row, but the cast-on and bind-off edges scallop in response to the groups of increases and decreases. Pam Allen's Tailored Scallops (page 56) use these uneven edges as a design element. You can make sharp points along the selvedge edge, as in Swatch 13 (Chart 13), by working yarnovers without decreases for several rows, then working all of the decreases at once as a series of bind-offs. This produces a sawtooth or pointed edging.

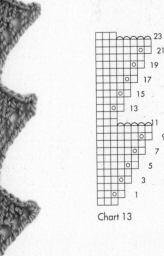
Chart 13

Swatch 13

See page 141 for chart symbol key.

Swatch 14

Swatch 15 (right side)

Swatch 15 (wrong side)

Swatch 16

OTHER WAYS TO GET LACE EFFECTS

You don't have to pair yarnovers with decreases to create lacy effects. An easy alternative is to use very large needles with very fine yarn. In Swatch 14, a fingering-weight yarn is worked in stockinette stitch on size 10½ (6.5 mm) needles. After blocking, the stitches open up to reveal an openwork pattern. This is the concept behind Mercedes Tarasovich-Clark's Retro Redux Shrug (page 74) and Annie Modesitt's Sterling and Crystal Cuff (page 121). By working only some of the rows with the larger needle, as in Swatch 15, you can get a striped effect. Sometimes these effects are best seen on wrong-side rows. Another way to produce the same effect is to wrap the yarn two or more times around the needle when making knit stitches. In Swatch 16 (Chart 16), the lozenge shapes are produced by wrapping the yarn around the needle one, two, three, two times, then one time on adjacent stitches. The extra wraps are dropped from the needle on the following row, producing groups of progressively longer, then shorter stitches. Finally, you can use dropped stitches to give a lacy effect. In Swatch 17 (Chart 17), every fourth stitch was dropped and raveled down to the cast-on edge. This is how Kat Coyle achieved the lace in her Show-Off Ruffle Skirt (page 94). In Swatch 18 (Chart 18), extra stitches were increased, worked for a few rows, then dropped and raveled down to the initial increases to produce lozenge-shaped motifs. You can play with the placement of the increases to get all kinds of different patterns.

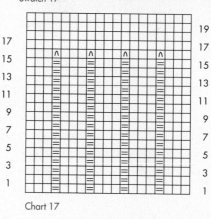

Swatch 17

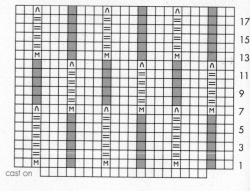

Swatch 18

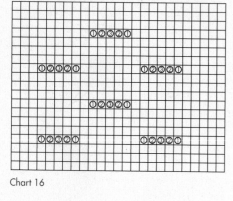

Chart 16

Chart 17

Chart 18

cast on

See page 141 for chart symbol key.

READING LACE CHARTS

Many knitters shrink at the sight of a charted pattern, intimidated by the seemingly complicated arrangement of seemingly arbitrary symbols. Once they've knitted from a chart, however, many find charts truly logical and easy to follow. Charts have several advantages over row-by-row knitting instructions written out in words: They let you see at a glance what's to be done and what the pattern will look like knitted; they help you recognize how the stitches and rows relate to one another; and they usually take up less space than written instructions.

Charts are a visual representation of the knitted fabric viewed from the right side, plotted on graph paper so that one square represents one stitch and one horizontal row represents one row of knitting. The symbols in the squares indicate how to work each stitch. Unless otherwise specified, when you're knitting in rows, you should read a chart from the bottom to the top; from right to left for right-side rows and from left to right for wrong-side rows. When knitting in the round (where the right side of the knitting is always facing you), read all rows from bottom to top and right to left.

SYMBOLS

Though not all publications use exactly the same symbols (for example, some use a horizontal dash to denote a purl stitch, others use a dot), for the most part, the symbols represent what the stitches look like when viewed from the right side of the knitting. Symbols that slant to the left represent left-slanting stitches. Symbols that slant to the right represent right-slanting stitches. Notice how the symbols in the charts on pages 136–139 mimic the stitches in the knitted swatches. The symbols show the stitch after it has been worked. Therefore, the symbol for k2tog occupies just one box, even though two stitches are used to perform that action. When a lace pattern causes the stitch count to vary from row to row, the edges of the chart will shift in and out accordingly, or the chart will indicate stitches that have been eliminated with a "no-stitch" symbol.

Because charts are presented as viewed from the right side only, some symbols represent two different maneuvers—one for right-side rows and another for wrong-side rows. For example, in stockinette stitch, stitches are knitted on right-side rows and purled on wrong-side rows. However, charted stockinette stitch shows only the right (knit) side. A list of the most common symbols and their right-and wrong-side definitions is shown below.

OOH LA LACE DRESS AND STOLE
shirley poden

Charts let you see at a glance how the stitches relate to each other in a lace pattern.

Symbol	Definition	Symbol	Definition	Symbol	Definition
☐	knit on RS; purl on WS	⋌	right double decrease	▩	no stitch
⊡	purl on RS; knit on WS	⋋	left double decrease	③	wrap yarn around needle number of times shown
⭕	yo	⌒	bind off 1 st	☐	pattern repeat
⟋	k2tog	⋀	drop 1 st		
⟍	ssk	═	laddered dropped st		
⋀	center double decrease	M	M1 increase		

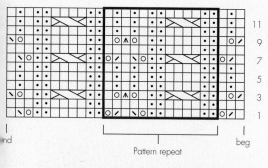

11
9
7
5
3
1

nd   beg

Pattern repeat

See page 141 for chart symbol key.

Row Numbers

Rows are numbered along the side of most charts. Row numbers appearing along the right edge denote right-side rows to be read from right to left. Row numbers appearing along the left edge denote wrong-side rows to be read from left to right. For example, if the number 1 is on the right edge of the chart, that and all subsequent odd-numbered rows are right-side rows; all even-numbered rows are worked from the wrong side (from left to right). With few exceptions, charts in this book designate Row 1 as a right-side row. For some patterns, this requires a "set-up row" to be worked prior to the first row of the chart to get the stitches in the necessary sequence of knits and purls before working the first right-side row.

Pattern Repeats

Charts generally show at least one pattern repeat. If the repeat is complex, more than one repeat may be charted to help you see how the individual motifs look adjacent to each other. In row-by-row instructions, pattern repeats are flanked by asterisks or square brackets. On charts, these repeated sections are outlined in heavy or colored boxes, or they're indicated by brackets or notes along lower or upper edge of the chart.

Centering Pattern Repeats

Some patterns that are worked back and forth in rows require extra stitches to center, or balance, a charted pattern. In row-by-row instructions, such patterns are reported as repeating over a multiple of a number of stitches plus extra stitches (i.e., balanced k2, p2 ribbing worked back and forth in rows is a multiple of 4 stitches plus 2). On charts, these extra balancing stitches appear at the right or left sides of the chart, with the repeat clearly marked in between. On right-side rows, work from right to left, working the stitches at the right edge once before the pattern repeat, then work the repeat as many times as necessary, and end by working the stitches at the left edge after the pattern repeat once. On wrong-side rows, work from left to right, working the stitches on the left edge once, work the repeat box as many times as necessary, and end by working the stitches on the right edge once.

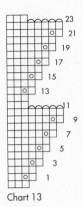

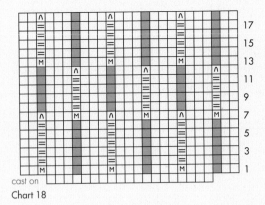

Chart 13

cast on

Chart 18

No Stitch

Many lace patterns involve increases or decreases that cause the stitch count to rise or fall, thereby requiring the number of boxes in a chart to vary from one row to the next. For some patterns, these variations are simply represented by uneven chart edges, as shown above. For other patterns, adding or subtracting boxes at the edge of a chart may disrupt the vertical stitch alignment. In these cases, a special symbol for "no stitch" is used to accommodate "missing" stitches while they maintain the vertical integrity of the pattern. In this book, missing stitches are represented by shaded boxes. When you come to a shaded box, simply skip over it and continue to the next stitch of the chart.

INCORPORATING LACE IN YOUR OWN DESIGN

It's not that difficult to incorporate a lace pattern into your own garment design, but be prepared to knit a few swatches to get the right combination of yarn, needles, and stitch pattern. Most designers favor using smooth yarns in solid colors for lace, but you can get beautiful effects by using a mohair yarn, as in Mari Lynn Patrick's Featherlight Lingerie Dress (page 40), a subtly variegated yarn, as in Pam Allen's Little Silk Shrug (page 46), or even wire, as in Annie Modesitt's Sterling and Crystal cuff (page 120). So that the stitches will have ample space to open up and show the full effect of a design when blocked, it's a good idea to knit lace patterns with needles a size or two larger than recommended for working the same yarn in stockinette stitch. To simplify your knitting, look for stitch patterns that work all the stitch manipulations (increases, decreases, etc.) on right-side rows, so that you can just knit or purl back on the wrong-side rows. Also consider the number of stitches in a pattern repeat. Garments look best if they're planned to use full pattern repeats without mismatched partial repeats at the seams. If you want a lace pattern to coincide with a cast-on or bind-off edge, be sure to use a very elastic cast-on or bind-off (see Tips for Working Lace, page 149) that will stretch with the lace pattern.

SHETLAND SHAWL TURNED VEST

véronik avery

Choose a lace pattern that has all of the increases and decreases worked on right-side rows only so you can simply knit or purl wrong-side rows.

CENTER A MOTIF

Most stitch dictionaries report stitch patterns as a specific number of stitches in a repeat with extra, balancing stitches. For example, the Miniature Wings pattern at left repeats over 19 stitches and has 1 extra stitch so that the pattern looks the same at each selvedge. To work full pattern repeats, plan to cast on a multiple of 19 stitches, then add 1 stitch for balance. However, if you want to work the same pattern in rounds, eliminate the balancing stitch so that only full repeats are worked.

Once you have decided on the yarn and stitch pattern, knit a generous swatch (at least 6" [15 cm] and/or two full pattern repeats square) and block it (see page 148) to open up the lace pattern and confirm that the yarn, stitch pattern, and needles give the feel and drape you're seeking. Measure the gauge (after blocking) to determine how many stitches you'll need to cast on to achieve the finished width you want. You may have to adjust this number to allow for full pattern repeats.

Many stitch patterns are directional and appear different depending on whether you hold them in the direction they were knitted or upside down, as in Shirley Paden's Ooh La Lace Stole (page 64) and Nancy Bush's Lily of the Valley Shawl (page 20). If you want the pattern to look the same on each end, work the piece in two sections that are joined at the center (by seaming, binding off the stitches together, or grafting) instead of working a single long strip. Doing so will make the two ends of the piece appear symmetrical. You could also begin the first half in the center with a provisional cast-on, work the first side, then pick up stitches from the base of the provisional cast-on to work the other side from the center outwards to match the first.

UNEVEN CAST-ON, BIND-OFF, AND SELVEDGE EDGES

When designing lace projects, take advantage of the uneven cast-on, bind-off, and selvedge edges formed by some lace patterns. Design your socks so that the scalloped cast-on edge is the at the top of the leg, as in Evelyn Clark's Floral Lace Anklets (page 26) or the hem of a garment, as in Pam Allen's Tailored Scallops (page 56). Or add edgings with zigzag edges to decorate otherwise straight edges of scarves, shawls, and garments, as in Nancy Bush's Lily of the Valley Shawl (page 20) and Mari Lynn Patrick's Just Right Wrap (page 12).

Miniature Wings

selvedge sts not shown

	k on RS; p on WS
•	p on RS; k on WS
╱	k2tog

╲	ssk
O	yo
	pattern repeat

SHAPING LACE PATTERNS

One of the biggest challenges when designing a lace garment is maintaining the balance of increases and decreases in the lace pattern while increasing or decreasing to shape the garment. The easiest solution is to avoid the problem altogether—design the piece so that the lace pattern is positioned where it won't interfere with shaping increases and decreases. For example, in Kat Coyle's Show-Off Ruffle Skirt (page 94), the lace pattern is completed before any shaping begins. Mari Lynn Patrick took a different approach in her Just Right Wrap (page 12) where she added the lace edging after the jacket was knitted and assembled, and in her Featherlight Lingerie Dress (page 40), where she picked up stitches at the base of the skirt and worked the narrow edging downward.

Another solution is to work the lace pattern only as long as full pattern repeats of the lace can be worked. As soon as the shaping encroaches on a repeat, discontinue working the lace pattern and work the stitches in the partial repeat in stockinette, garter, or another background stitch pattern. The disadvantage to this method is that the lace pattern, especially ones that repeat over a large number of stitches, can have a jagged edge where the background stitch pattern meets the lace. You can minimize this to a large degree, as Kathy Zimmerman did when shaping the armholes and neck in the Katharine Hepburn Cardigan (page 78), by working as much of the lace pattern repeat as possible, only shifting to the background stitch pattern when there are not enough stitches to make both the yarnover and decrease of a pair.

Although not suitable for shaping armholes and necks, a clever alternative is to change needle size to cause a piece to narrow or widen. Shirley Paden used this trick to shape the hips, waist, and bust of her Ooh La Lace Dress (page 64), changing to larger needles for the hip and bust areas and smaller needles for the waist. Lisa Daehlin used the same approach to increase the calf circumference in her Leg Cozies (page 100).

For an excellent detailed discussion on how to maintain lace patterns while working shaping increases or decreases, see Eunny Jang's article "Beyond the Basics: Lace—Shaping Your Garment" in the Fall 2006 issue of *Interweave Knits*.

SHOW-OFF RUFFLE SKIRT
kat coyle

Change needle size to cause a piece to narrow or widen.

LEG COZIES
lisa daehlin

It's not unusual to make mistakes when knitting lace, but many of these mistakes are easy to fix.

COMMON MISTAKES AND EASY FIXES

Lace patterns present plenty of opportunities to make mistakes—by missing a yarnover or decrease or by working the yarnover or decrease in the wrong place. Although you may not realize your mistake at the time, you'll usually notice something's wrong when you work the following pattern row.

MISSED YARNOVER

Let's say, for example, that you forgot to make the yarnover on Row 7 of the chart below and you don't notice a problem until you find that you're a stitch short on Row 9. To fix the problem, work in pattern to where the missing yarnover should be (Figure 1), use another needle or a crochet hook to pick up the horizontal strand from Row 7 from where the yarnover should have been made (Figure 2), loop the horizontal strand from Row 8 through this loop (Figure 3), place the new stitch on the left needle (Figure 4), and continue as charted. The replaced yarnover will be a little smaller than the others, but the difference will be barely noticeable after the piece has been blocked.

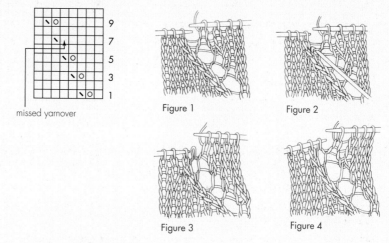

missed yarnover

Figure 1

Figure 2

Figure 3

Figure 4

EXTRA YARNOVER

Let's say that when working the same chart you made the opposite mistake—you made a yarnover on Row 5 where none was required and don't notice it until you're working Row 7. To fix this mistake, work Row 7 in pattern to where the extra yarnover is (Figure 1), drop this extra stitch and let it ravel down to the initial yarnover on Row 5 (Figure 2), and continue as charted. The stitches around the dropped yarnover will appear a bit looser than the others, but again, the difference will be negligible after the piece has been blocked.

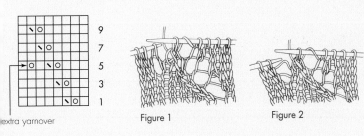

extra yarnover

Figure 1   Figure 2

MISSED DECREASE

Now, let's see what happens if you miss the decrease on Row 5—instead of working two stitches as a ssk decrease on Row 5, you knitted them. On the next right-side row (Row 7) you notice that you have too many stitches and the prominent line formed by the decreases is missing. In this case, you'd work Row 7 to where the decrease should have been made (Figure 1), drop both stitches down two rows (Figure 2), pick them up together as ssk (Figure 3), then use another needle or crochet hook to pick up the horizontal strand of Row 6 through the new decreased stitch (Figure 4), place this stitch on the left needle, and continue as charted. If the missing decrease were a k2tog, you'd follow the same steps: first work in pattern to where the decrease should have been (Figure 5), drop both stitches down two rows (Figure 6), and pick them together as k2tog (Figure 7). If you missed a double decrease, you'd follow the same steps, but drop the three stitches that should have been involved in the decrease and rework them as the appropriate type of double decrease. Although the resulting stitch will be a bit looser than the surrounding ones, the size of the stitches will even out considerably after blocking.

LITTLE SILK SHRUG

pam allen

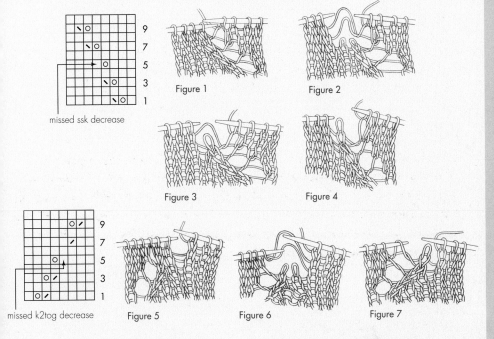

missed ssk decrease

Figure 1   Figure 2

Figure 3   Figure 4

missed k2tog decrease

Figure 5   Figure 6   Figure 7

Count stitches
after every pattern
row to make
sure you haven't
inadvertently
added or missed
a yarnover
or decrease.

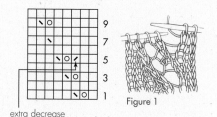

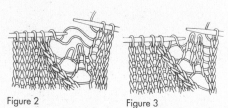

extra decrease

Figure 1

EXTRA DECREASE

It's possible that you'll work an extra decrease in a lace pattern. If this is the case, work to where the extra decrease was worked (Figure 1), drop that stitch down to the row that the erroneous decrease was made (Figure 2), pick up the two stitches (Figure 3), and continue in pattern as charted.

WRONG TYPE OF DECREASE

It's not uncommon to work the wrong type of decrease—a left-slanting ssk instead of a right-slanting k2tog, or vice versa. Fortunately, you'll notice that the defining line of the decrease is off-kilter on the next right-side row. When this happens, work to the stitch directly over the decreased stitch, drop this stitch down through the row where the wrong decrease was made, pick up the two stitches following the correct decrease method, and continue in pattern as charted.

Figure 2   Figure 3

BLOCKING

No lace pattern is complete until it has been blocked. For best results, thoroughly wet the piece by submerging it in room-temperature water. Gently squeeze out the water (taking particular care not to twist or wring the piece), then blot out more moisture by rolling it in clean bath towels. The more water you remove now, the sooner the piece will dry.

Lay the damp piece on a clean towel or sheet on a flat surface (a bed or padded rug works well for large pieces such as shawls). Beginning at the center, gently pull the piece both vertically and horizontally until the openwork pattern is revealed and the piece is evenly stretched to the desired dimensions. Place a yardstick alongside the piece, if necessary, to help you maintain even edges. If using blocking wires, thread them through the straight edges of the lace piece or through every point or scallop, then use pins to anchor the wires with the lace stretched uniformly in all directions (Figure 1). If you don't have blocking wires, use rust-proof pins to pin the piece to shape, placing a pin at every corner or point in the pattern (Figure 2). Alternatively, you can thread a long length of smooth cotton string through each corner or point, then tie the ends of the string together and use pins to stretch out the string (Figure 3), stretching the knitting as you do so. Be sure to thread the string in the same direction through all of the points (i.e., always from front to back or vice versa) to get the most uniform result. No matter which method you use to pin out the lace pattern, allow 24 hours for it to thoroughly air-dry. Although the surface of the yarn may feel dry to the touch, you want to be sure that the yarn has dried all the way through before removing the pins.

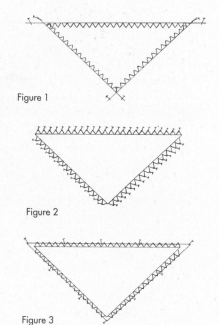

Figure 1

Figure 2

Figure 3

TIPS FOR WORKING LACE

❖ To ensure that the cast-on edge will stretch along with the lace pattern, choose a very elastic cast-on. Good choices are the Old Norwegian and knitted methods, both of which are illustrated in the Glossary on pages 152 and 153. You may also want to make sure that you allow enough space (¼" [6 mm] is good) between stitches as you cast them onto the needle. This will give a little more widthwise stretch between the stitches that will translate into a more elastic edge.

❖ Likewise, to ensure that the bind-off edge will stretch along with the lace pattern, use a flexible bind-off. Both the sewn method and the suspended method (see Glossary, page 151) are worked with extra yarn that gives the edge additional stretch.

❖ Use stitch markers to separate individual pattern repeats, particularly if you're working a complicated lace pattern. The markers will alert you when you're at the end of a repeat, and if the stitches on your needles don't line up with the chart, or if you don't have the correct number of stitches between the markers, you'll only have to rip back stitches for the last repeat to correct the mistake.

❖ It's a good idea to count stitches after every pattern row to make sure you haven't inadvertently added or missed a yarnover or decrease. Counting stitches will also give you a chance to look at your work and identify problems such as misplaced yarnovers or decreases, or decreases that were worked with the wrong slant.

❖ Make sure you have good light when knitting lace patterns. You want to see the individual stitches and their manipulations clearly. If you're working with dark yarn, spread a light-colored towel across your lap so that the work will be easier to see.

❖ Don't knit lace patterns, particularly complicated ones, when you're tired or have a lot of distractions. It's all too easy to loose count and make errors. If necessary, turn off your phone and seclude yourself in a quiet room.

❖ If at all possible, avoid putting down your knitting in the middle of a row. Not only do you run the risk of forgetting where you are in the pattern repeat, but stitches, particularly yarnovers, can slip off the needles and ravel down a few rows before you pick up the needles again.

❖ Use a "lifeline" to reduce the number of rows you may have to rip out if you do make a mistake and to ensure that you pick up all the stitches correctly when you return the stitches to the needle. A lifeline is a length of smooth contrasting thread that is inserted through a correct row of stitches on the needle. If you notice a mistake in a subsequent row, you can rip back to the lifeline where you know the pattern is correct. To insert a lifeline, thread smooth contrasting yarn on a tapestry needle and draw it through the bottom of every stitch on the needle, taking care not to thread it through any markers, and leaving long tails hanging at each selvedge edge (Figure 1). Keeping the lifeline out of the way, continue knitting the pattern as established (Figure 2). In the unhappy event that you discover a mistake in a subsequent row, rip out the knitting to the row above the lifeline, then rip out the row held by the lifeline one stitch at a time (Figure 3), placing the stitches on a needle (it helps to use a much smaller needle than your main needle for this) as you go. Keep the lifeline in place (in case you need it again), and continue knitting the pattern. Depending on the complexity of the pattern and your aversion to ripping out your knitting, insert lifelines every two to twelve inches (5 to 30.5 cm).

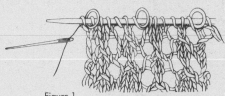

Figure 1

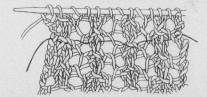

Figure 2

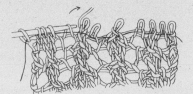

Figure 3

ABBREVIATIONS

beg	begin; begins; beginning
bet	between
BO	bind off
cont	continue; continues; continuing
CC	contrast color
cm	centimeter(s)
cn	cable needle
CO	cast on
dec(s)	decrease(s); decreasing
dpn	double-pointed needles
foll	follow; follows; following
g	gram(s)
inc(s)	increase(s); increasing
k	knit
k1f&b	knit into the front and back of same st
kwise	knitwise, as if to knit
m	marker(s)
MC	main color
mm	millimeter(s)
M1	make one (increase)
p	purl
p1f&b	purl into front and back of same st
patt(s)	pattern(s)
psso	pass slipped st over

p2sso	pass 2 slipped stitches over
pwise	purlwise, as if to purl
rem	remain; remains; remaining
rep	repeat(s)
rev St st	reverse stockinette stitch
rnd(s)	round(s)
RS	right side
sl	slip
sl st	slip st (slip 1 st pwise unless otherwise indicated)
ssk	slip, slip, knit (decrease)
st(s)	stitch(es)
St st	stockinette stitch
tbl	through back loop
tog	together
WS	wrong side
wyb	with yarn in back
wyf	with yarn in front
yd	yard(s)
yo	yarnover
*	repeat starting point
* *	repeat all instructions between asterisks
( )	alternate measurements and/or instructions
[ ]	work instructions as a group a specified number of times

BIND-OFFS

Sewn Bind-Off

Cut yarn three times the width of the knitting to be bound off, and thread onto a tapestry needle. Working from right to left, *insert tapestry needle purlwise (from right to left) through first two stitches (Figure 1) and pull yarn through. Bring tapestry needle knitwise (from left to right) through first stitch (Figure 2), pull yarn through, and slip this stitch off knitting needle. Repeat from *.

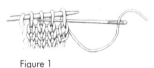

Figure 1

Figure 2

Standard Bind-Off

Knit the first stitch, *knit the next stitch (2 stitches on right needle), insert left needle tip into first stitch on right needle (Figure 1) and lift this stitch up and over the second stitch (Figure 2) and off the needle (Figure 3). Repeat from * for the desired number of stitches.

Figure 1

Figure 2

Figure 3

Suspended Bind-Off

Slip one stitch, knit one stitch, *insert left needle tip into first stitch on right needle and lift the first stitch over the second, keeping the lifted stitch at the end of the left needle (Figure 1). Skipping the lifted stitch, knit the next stitch (Figure 2), then slip both stitches off the left needle—two stitches remain on right needle and one stitch has been bound off (Figure 3). Repeat from * until no stitches remain on left needle, then pass first stitch on right needle over second.

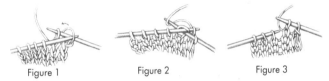

Figure 1

Figure 2

Figure 3

Three-Needle Bind-Off

Place the stitches to be joined onto two separate needles and hold the needles parallel so that the right sides of knitting face together. Insert a third needle into the first stitch on each of two needles (Figure 1) and knit them together as one stitch (Figure 2), *knit the next stitch on each needle the same way, then use the left needle tip to lift the first stitch over the second and off the needle (Figure 3). Repeat from * until no stitches remain on the left needles. Cut yarn and pull tail through last stitch to secure.

Figure 1

Figure 2

Figure 3

CAST-ONS

Backward Loop CO

*Loop working yarn and place it on needle backward so that it doesn't unwind. Repeat from *.

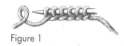

Figure 1

Cable Cast-On

Hold needle with working yarn in your left hand with the wrong side of the work facing you. *Insert right needle *between* the first two stitches on left needle (Figure 1), wrap yarn around needle as if to knit, draw yarn through (Figure 2), and place new loop on left needle (Figure 3) to form a new stitch. Repeat from * for the desired number of stitches, always working between the first two stitches on the left needle.

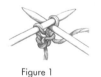

Figure 1   Figure 2   Figure 3

Crochet Chain Provisional Cast-On

With waste yarn and crochet hook, make a loose crochet chain (see page 154) about four stitches more than you need to cast on. With knitting needle, working yarn, and beginning two stitches from end of chain, pick up and knit one stitch through the back loop of each crochet chain (Figure 1) for desired number of stitches. When you're ready to work in the opposite direction, pull out the crochet chain to expose live stitches (Figure 2).

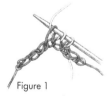 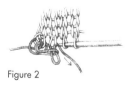

Figure 1   Figure 2

Provisional (Invisible) Cast-On

Make a loose slipknot of working yarn and place it on the right needle. Hold a length of waste yarn next to the slipknot and around your left thumb; hold working yarn over your left index finger. *Bring right needle forward under waste yarn, over working yarn, grab a loop of working yarn (Figure 1), then bring needle back behind the working yarn and grab a second loop (Figure 2). Repeat from * for the desired number of stitches. When you're ready to work in the opposite direction, place the exposed loops on a knitting needle as you pull out the waste yarn.

 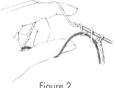

Figure 1   Figure 2

Knitted Cast-On

Make a slipknot of working yarn and place it on the left needle if there are no stitches already there. *Use the right needle to knit the first stitch (or slipknot) on left needle (Figure 1) and place new loop onto left needle to form a new stitch (Figure 2). Repeat from * for the desired number of stitches, always knitting into the last stitch made.

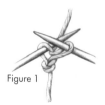 

Figure 1   Figure 2

Long-Tail (Continental) Cast-On

Leaving a long tail (about ½" [1.3 cm] for each stitch to be cast on), make a slipknot and place on right needle. Place thumb and index finger of your left hand between the yarn ends so that working yarn is around your index finger and tail end is around your thumb, and secure the yarn ends with your other fingers. Hold your palm upwards, making a V of yarn (Figure 1). *Bring needle up through loop on thumb (Figure 2), catch first strand around index finger, and go back down through loop on thumb (Figure 3). Drop loop off thumb and, placing thumb back in V configuration, tighten resulting stitch on needle (Figure 4). Repeat from * for the desired number of stitches.

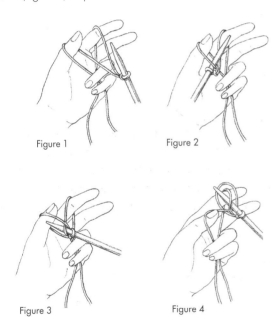

Figure 1   Figure 2

Figure 3   Figure 4

Old Norwegian Cast-On

Leaving a long tail, make a slipknot and place on right needle. Place thumb and index finger between yarn ends so that the working yarn is around your index finger and the tail is around your thumb. Secure the ends with your other fingers and hold your palm upward, making a V of yarn (Figure 1). *Bring needle in front of thumb, under both yarns around thumb, down into center of thumb loop, forward again, and over top of yarn around index finger (Figure 2), catch this yarn, and bring needle back down through thumb loop (Figure 3), turning thumb slightly to make room for needle to pass through. Drop loop off thumb (Figure 4) and place thumb back in V configuration while tightening up resulting stitch on needle. Repeat from * for desired number of stitches.

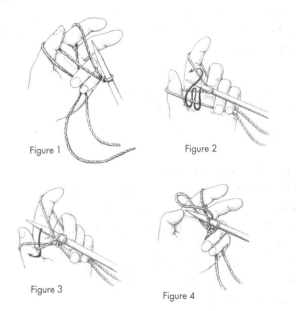

Figure 1   Figure 2

Figure 3   Figure 4

CROCHET

Crochet Chain (ch)

Make a slipknot and place it on crochet hook.
*Yarn over hook and draw through loop on hook.
Repeat from * for the desired number of stitches.
To fasten off, cut yarn and draw end through last
loop formed.

Reverse Single Crochet (shrimp st)

Working from left to right, insert hook into a stitch, draw through a
loop, bring yarn over hook, and draw it through the first one. *Insert
hook into next stitch to the right (Figure 1), draw through a loop, bring
yarn over hook again (Figure 2), and draw it through both loops on
hook (Figure 3). Repeat from * for the desired number of stitches.

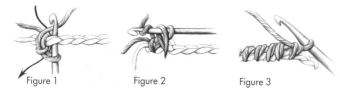

Figure 1   Figure 2   Figure 3

Single Crochet (sc)

*Insert hook into the second chain from the hook or into the next
stitch, yarn over hook and draw through a loop, yarn over hook (Figure 1), and draw it through both loops on hook (Figure 2). Repeat
from * for the desired number of stitches.

Figure 1   Figure 2

Slip Stitch Crochet (sl st)

*Insert hook into stitch, yarn over hook and draw a loop through
both the stitch and loop already on hook. Repeat from * for the
desired number of stitches.

DECREASES

P2tog Through Back Loops (p2togtbl)

Bring right needle tip behind 2 stitches on left needle, enter through
the back loop of the second stitch, then the first stitch, then purl them
together.

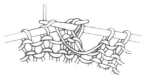

Ssk

Slip 2 stitches individually knitwise (Figure 1), insert left needle tip
into the fronts of these 2 slipped stitches, and use the right needle to
knit them together through their back loops (Figure 2).

Figure 1   Figure 2

Ssp

Holding yarn in front, slip 2 stitches individually knitwise (Figure 1),
then slip these 2 stitches back onto left needle (they will be turned
on the needle), and purl them together through their back loops
(Figure 2).

Figure 1   Figure 2

GRAFTING

Kitchener Stitch

Arrange stitches on two needles so that there is the same number of stitches on each needle. Hold the needles parallel to each other with right sides of the knitting facing up. Allowing about ½" (1.3 cm) per stitch to be grafted, thread matching yarn on a tapestry needle. Work from right to left as follows:

Step 1. Bring tapestry needle through the first stitch on the front needle as if to purl and leave the stitch on the needle (Figure 1).

Step 2. Bring tapestry needle through the first stitch on the back needle as if to knit and leave that stitch on the needle (Figure 2).

Step 3. Bring tapestry needle through the first front stitch as if to knit and slip this stitch off the needle, then bring tapestry needle through the next front stitch as if to purl and leave this stitch on the needle (Figure 3).

Step 4. Bring tapestry needle through the first back stitch as if to purl and slip this stitch off the needle, then bring tapestry needle through the next back stitch as if to knit and leave this stitch on the needle (Figure 4).

Repeat Steps 3 and 4 until no stitches remain on the needles, adjusting the tension to match the rest of the knitting as you go.

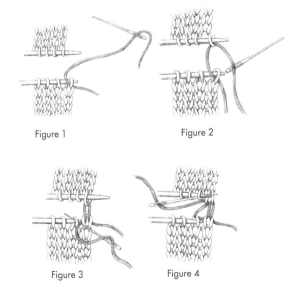

Figure 1   Figure 2

Figure 3   Figure 4

I-CORD

Using 2 double-pointed needles, cast on the desired number of stitches (usually 3 to 4). *Without turning the work, slide stitches to other end of needle, pull the yarn around the back, and knit the stitches as usual. Repeat from * for desired length, always with the right side of the work facing you.

INCREASES

K1f&b

Knit into a stitch but leave it on the left needle (Figure 1), then knit through the back loop of the same stitch (Figure 2) and slip the original stitch off the needle.

Figure 1   Figure 2

Raised (M1) Increase

Note: If no direction of slant is specified, use the left slant.

Left Slant (M1L): With left needle tip, lift the strand between last knitted stitch and first stitch on left needle from front to back (Figure 1), then knit the lifted loop through the back (Figure 2).

Figure 1   Figure 2

Right Slant (M1R): With left needle tip, lift the strand between the needles from back to front (Figure 1). Knit the lifted loop through the front (Figure 2).

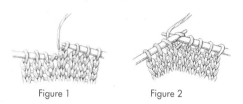

Figure 1   Figure 2

P1f&b

Purl into a stitch but leave it on the left needle (Figure 1), then purl through the back loop of the same stitch (Figure 2), and slip the original stitch off the needle.

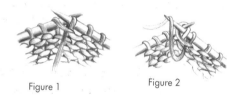

Figure 1   Figure 2

PICK UP AND PURL

With purl side of work facing and working from right to left, *insert needle tip under selvedge stitch from the far side to the near side, wrap yarn around needle purlwise (Figure 1), and pull loop through (Figure 2). Repeat from *.

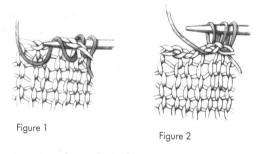

Figure 1   Figure 2

SHORT-ROWS

Work to turning point, slip next stitch purlwise to right needle, then bring the yarn to the front (Figure 1). Slip the same stitch back to the left needle (Figure 2), turn the work around and bring the yarn in position for the next stitch, wrapping the slipped stitch with working yarn as you do so. When you come to a wrapped stitch on a subsequent row, hide the wrap by working it together with the wrapped stitch as follows: Insert right needle tip under the wrap (from the front if wrapped stitch is a knit stitch; from the back if wrapped stitch is a purl stitch), then into the stitch on the needle, and work the stitch and its wrap together as a single stitch.

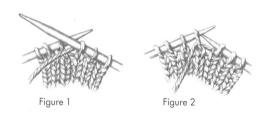

Figure 1   Figure 2

CONTRIBUTING DESIGNERS

Pam Allen is the editor in chief of *Interweave Knits* and author *of Knitting for Dummies* and *Scarf Style*, and coauthor of *Wrap Style*. After twenty-five years designing handknits, she still learns something new on a regular basis.

Véronik Avery is the creative director for JCA Yarns. She has been designing for just four years and is currently working on her first book, *Knitting Classic Styles*, due out in 2007. Véronik lives in Montreal, Quebec, with her husband and daughter.

Nancy Bush is the author of *Folk Socks, Folk Knitting in Estonia, Knitting on the Road*, and *Knitting Vintage Socks*, and is currently working on a book of Estonian lace patterns. Nancy is also owner of The Wooly West, a mail-order knitting shop (www.woolywest.com) in Salt Lake City, Utah.

Evelyn A. Clark lives in the Pacific Northwest where she delights in living a simple life and knitting as often as possible. She is passionate about knitting socks and lace, and combining the two whenever possible.

Kat Coyle learned the basics of knitting from her mother at the fine age of eight years old. Kat is currently working on a book of bohemian-inspired designs for small children, due out in fall 2007.

Lisa Daehlin lives in New York City where she is an opera singer, milliner, and knitter. She draws inspiration from the architecture, people, and energy of diverse cultures. Lisa teaches at the Cooper Union for the Advancement of Science and Art.

Norah Gaughan is the design director for Berroco Yarns and author of *Knitting Na-*

ture: 39 Designs Inspired by Patterns in Nature. In many of her designs she highlights a simple shape with an organically influenced focal point.

Priscilla Gibson-Roberts is passionate about traditional knitting and spinning techniques and has written a number of books on the topic, including *Knitting in the Old Way, Spinning in the Old Way, Ethnic Socks & Stockings, Simple Socks: Plain and Fancy*, and *Salish Indian Sweaters*.

Annie Modesitt has a background in costume design that radiates throughout her knitting designs. She is the author of *Confessions of a Knitting Heretic, Knitted Millinery, Men Who Knit and the Dogs Who Love Them*, and *Twist & Loop, Dozens of Jewelry Designs to Knit and Crochet with Wire*. Visit her website at www .anniemodesitt.com.

Michele Rose Orne has been designing knitwear for the garment industry and yarn companies for more than twenty years. She enjoys translating textures, colors, and shapes from nature to fashion runways into knittable designs. Michele is working on her first book due out in fall 2008.

Shirley Paden lives in New York City where she operates Shirley Paden Custom Knits and teaches a series of master knitting classes for people working in the fashion industry. Shirley also conducts traveling teaching seminars on lace, color knitting, entrelac knitting, cables, and finishing.

Mari Lynn Patrick studied knitwear design at a guild school in Leicester, England, in the early 1970s. Since then she has been a prolific crochet and knitwear designer for

magazines and yarn companies. She lives in Baltimore, Maryland.

Mona Schmidt lives in Montreal, Quebec, and is the associate creative director of JCA Inc. Visit her blog www.knitstricken.blogspot.com.

Vicki Square is passionate about knitting. She is author of *Folk Bags, Folk Hats*, and that essential little book, *The Knitter's Companion*, which she revised in 2006. Vicki is currently working on a book of knitted kimonos, due out in fall 2007.

Mercedes Tarasovich-Clark has a degree in textiles from the Savannah College of Art and Design and is owner of Knit Nouveau, a yarn shop in Birmingham, Alabama. Visit her at www.knitnouveau.com.

Lois S. Young has been designing knitwear since 1977. She recently retired as a university calculus instructor. Lois is inspired by new patterns, especially lace, and her love of textiles. She credits Elizabeth Zimmermann and Meg Swanson for all of her knitting engineering skills.

Kathy Zimmerman, dubbed The Cable Queen by customers at her yarn shop Kathy's Kreations in Ligonier, Pennsylvania, is always looking for ways to incorporate cables in her knitwear designs. She thanks Eleanor Swogger for her help swatching and test knitting the Katharine Hepburn Cardigan.

Laura Zukaite is a native of Lithuania and is now pursuing a degree in fashion design at Parsons School of Design in New York City. When Laura isn't studying, she helps out at Sticks and Strings, a yarn shop in Scarsdale, New York.

BIBLIOGRAPHY

Abbey, Barbara. *Barbara Abbey's Knitting Lace.* Pittsville, Wisconsin: Schoolhouse Press, 1993.
> A collection of predominantly lace edging patterns from the late 1800s.

Erickson-Schweitzer, Jackie. "A Primer on Knitted Lace," in *Interweave Knits,* Summer 2006.
> A good introduction to knitted lace.

Jang, Eunny. Lace: "Shaping Your Garment," in *Interweave Knits,* Fall 2006.
> A valuable resource on how to maintain lace patterns during garment shaping.

Khmeleva, Galina, and Carol R. Noble. *Gossamer Webs: The History and Techniques of Orenburg Lace Shawls.* Loveland, Colorado: Interweave Press, 1998.
> Details every step in knitting intricate Russian shawls plus a dictionary of lace patterns.

Kinzel, Marianne. *First Book of Modern Lace Knitting* and *Second Book of Modern Lace Knitting.* New York: Dover, 1972.
> Lace patterns for mostly doilies and tablecloths that translate well into other projects.

Lewis, Susanna. *Knitting Lace: A Workshop with Patterns and Projects.* Newtown, Connecticut: Taunton Press, 1992.
> Out-of-print reference providing charts and instructions for ninety vintage lace patterns and explaining the fundamentals of lace construction.

Miller, Sharon. *Heirloom Knitting.* Lerwick: The Shetland Times Ltd., 2001.
> Instructions and charts for dozens of Shetland lace patterns.

Nehring, Nancy. *The Lacy Knitting of Mary Schiffmann.* Loveland, Colorado: Interweave Press, 1998.
> Lace patterns and life stories from the founding member of the Lacy Knitters Guild.

Swansen, Meg. *A Gathering of Lace.* Sioux Falls, South Dakota: XRX Books, 2000 and 2005.
> A collection of traditional lace designs from thirty-four contributors.

Stove, Margaret. *Creating Original Hand-Knitted Lace.* Berkeley, California: Lacis Publications, 1995.
> Solid information on lace theory and structure as well as instructions for creating and charting your own lace pattern.

Walker, Barbara. *A Treasury of Knitting Patterns* and *A Second Treasury of Knitting Patterns.* Pittsville, Wisconsin: Schoolhouse Press, 1998.
> Both volumes includes lace stitch patterns that you can mix and match into your own designs.

Waterman, Martha. *Traditional Knitted Lace Shawls.* Loveland, Colorado: Interweave Press, 1998.
> Everything you need to design and knit a triangular, square, circular, and half-circular shawl.

Wiseman, Nancie M. *Lace from the Attic: A Victorian Notebook of Knitted Lace Patterns.* Loveland, Colorado: Interweave Press, 1998.
> A collection of one woman's lace samples and knitting instructions.

Alchemy Yarns of Transformation
PO Box 1080
Sebastopol, CA 95473
www.alchemyyarns.com

Alpaca With a Twist
4272 Evans Jacobi Rd.
Georgetown, IN 47122
www.AlpacaWithATwist.com

Berroco Inc.
PO Box 367
14 Elmdale Rd.
Uxbridge, MA 01569
www.berroco.com
In Canada: S. R. Kertzer Ltd.

Blue Sky Alpacas Inc.
PO Box 88
Cedar, MN 55011
www.blueskyalpacas.com

Classic Elite Yarns
122 Western Ave.
Lowell, MA 01851
www.classiceliteyarns.com

Diamond Yarn
9697 St. Laurent, Ste. 101
Montreal, QC
Canada H3L 2N1
and
115 Martin Ross, Unit 3
Toronto, ON
Canada M3J 2L9
www.diamondyarn.com

Habu Textiles
135 W. 29th St., Ste. 804
New York, NY 10001
www.habutextiles.com

JaggerSpun
Box 188
Springvale, ME 04083
www.jaggerspun.com

JCA Inc./Reynolds
35 Scales Ln.
Townsend, MA 01469
www.jcacrafts.com

S.R. Kertzer Ltd.
50 Trowers Rd.
Woodbridge, ON
Canada L4L 7K6
www.kertzer.com

KnitPicks
13118 N.E. 4th St.
Vancouver, WA 98684
www.knitpicks.com

La Lana Wools
136-C Paseo del Pueblo Norte
Taos, NM 87571
www.lalanawools.com

Louet Sales
808 Commerce Park Dr.
Ogdensburg, NY 13669
www.louet.com

In Canada:
RR #4
Prescott, ON K0E 1T0

Muench Yarns Inc./GGH
1323 Scott St.
Petaluma CA 94954
www.muenchyarns.com
In Canada:
Les fils Muench
5640 Rue Valcourt
Brossard, QC J4W 1C5

Plymouth Yarn Co.
PO Box 28
Bristol, PA 19007
www.plymouthyarn.com

**Skacel Collection Inc./Sirdar/
Scheiller & Stahl**
PO Box 88110
Seattle, WA 98138
www.skacelknitting.com

Tahki/Stacy Charles/Filatura di Crosa
70 – 30 80th St., Bldg 36
Ridgewood, NY 11385
www.tahkistacycharles.com
In Canada: Diamond Yarn

Westminster Fibers/Regia/Rowan
4 Townsend West, Unit 8
Nashua, NH 03063
www.knitrowan.com
In Canada: Diamond Yarn

INDEX